£1.

THREE-LINE QUIPS

THREE-LINE QUIPS

Wisdom and Humour from Westminster

Selected and introduced by
EDWINA CURRIE, MP
with
STEPHEN PARKER
and **Clare Whelan**

Illustrated by
Sally Townsend

ASHFORD, BUCHAN & ENRIGHT
LEATHERHEAD

First published in 1992 by
Ashford, Buchan & Enright, Publishers
31 Bridge Street, Leatherhead, Surrey KT22 8BN

British Library Cataloguing in Publication Data
Currie, Edwina
Three-Line Quips: Wit and Humour from Westminster
I. Title II. Townsend, Sally
082

ISBN 1-85253-272-6

Typeset by Priory Publications, Haywards Heath
Printed in Great Britain by
FotoDirect Ltd, Brighton

CONTENTS

The Authors wish to record their thanks to Jonathan Metcalf
for his inspired contribution of the title for *Three-Line Quips*.

THE PRIME MINISTER

It is the task of politicians to communicate with
as much skill and fluency as they can muster. If
wit, innuendo and humour are added, the result can
be memorable - and quotable.

With Churchill, I am sure that there is much to
learn from other people's wise words. I welcome
"Three-Line Quips" and hope it will bring much
pleasure to all who read it.

John Major

September, 1992

INTRODUCTION

"We'd Like a Quote . . ."

by Edwina Currie, MP

When Stephen Parker approached me and asked if I would help with a collection of parliamentary anecdotes and quotations, I accepted with alacrity. He was the compiler, with my colleague Greg Knight, MP, of the collection which became *Westminster Words: Wit and Comment from Both Houses of Parliament* (Buchan & Enright, 1988). In the course of wide reading as a history teacher he comes across and collects many gems from letters and speeches, illustrating with their wit and wisdom the timeless thrills and foibles of the political world. Today, the memorable word is just as likely to be offered off the cuff to a journalist; the sort who phones in the middle of a meeting, saying casually, "We'd like a quote...."

All the items in this book were uttered by members of either the House of Commons or the House of Lords, though not necessarily during debates. We have included a few parliamentary spouses, where their remarks have thrown light on the life we and our families lead; and it is our hope that most of the quotations will be new and have not appeared in other recent collections.

Our thanks are due to Clare Whelan, and she is grateful to John, Fenton and Bridget for not minding so many hours spent at the word-processor instead of with them. Stephen Parker wishes to acknowledge with thanks John Evans, Giles Marshall and Patrick Pordage for their valuable assistance.

Our wish for all of you is that you may find here just that quote you were looking for. Should you claim it unattributed and as your own work, you may find your name in our next edition....

EDWINA CURRIE
Westminster, July 1992

1

CHAPTER ONE

Knife in the Back

Politics can be a very cruel game, with the sharpest thrusts coming from those whom one might really have expected to be friends and colleagues.

The story is told to every MP of a newly arrived chap, fresh from winning his election, sitting bright and eager on the green benches and raring to go. To an old hand nearby he says, "I can't wait to have a go at the enemy", and gesticulates to the other side. "Make no mistake, lad," intones the veteran, "them over there's the Opposition. The enemy is behind you."

Otherwise mild men reveal irritation with the task in hand (Baldwin), or the colleagues fate has created (Steel on Owen, Lloyd George on Asquith, Wilson on Benn). Tony Benn, however, has all too accurate a view of the weapons used against politicians by the press. For some of us, whatever we do or say will be reported in the worst possible light — not that politicians ever needed an excuse to feel sorry for themselves.

Just as often, late at night, members of the same party exchange pleasantries with a barbed edge. During the debate on fluoridation in 1985, Mr (now Sir) Nicholas Fairbairn was a fierce opponent, while I, having been involved with the NHS for some years, was a firm supporter. Nicholas was at pains to prove that fluoride was a poison and therefore should be kept out of water supplies.

"But could I point out to my Honourable Friend," I intervened, "that almost anything is a poison if taken in sufficient quantity, and that the amount of fluoride to be added is minute? If, for example, we were to spreadeagle the Honourable Member on the floor of this House, and pour sufficient water into him, then it would kill him very quickly."

He fixed me with a baleful glare. "I cannot imagine what would be worse," he said, "being spreadeagled by the Honourable Lady or having all that unadulterated pure water poured down my throat."

Herbert Henry Asquith, 1st Earl of Oxford and Asquith (1852-1928)

"One to mislead the public, another to mislead the Cabinet and the third to mislead itself." (On being told that the War Office kept three sets of figures.)
Alistair Horne, *The Price of Glory* , Chapter 2

Baroness Asquith (Lady Violet Bonham Carter) (1887-1969)

"Bonar Law never led his Party. He was always looking over his shoulder to see if he was being followed."
The Times, 2 November 1964

Nancy, Lady Astor (1879-1964)

Lady Astor had little respect for the dilution of the aristocracy, observing that "Anyone's blood can become blue for a lump sum down".
Memoirs

"Grass is growing on the Front Bench."
Observer, 1953

Stanley Baldwin, 1st Earl Baldwin of Bewdley (1867-1947)

"I can quite understand why people were put in the Tower in the old days and I would quite gladly put Mrs Simpson there if I could."

Lord Beaverbrook (William Maxwell Aitken, 1st Baron Beaverbrook) (1879-1964)

"Lloyd George did not seem to care which way he travelled provided he was in the driver's seat."

Aneurin Bevan (1897-1960)

"As one bastard to another, I accept your apology." (To Hugh Dalton in 1946.)

"The hero's need of the people outlasts their need of him." (Of Churchill in February 1944.)

Anthony Wedgwood Benn (1925-   )

"If I rescued a child from drowning the Press would no doubt headline the story 'Benn grabs child'."
Observer, 2 March 1975

Barbara Castle (Baroness Castle of Blackburn) (1911-   )

"Why get rid of Chamberlain to put in Halifax? It's like getting rid of the organ-grinder to put in the monkey."
Martin Gilbert, *Churchill*, BBC1, January 1992

Lord Hugh Cecil, 1st Baron Quickswood (1869-1956)

"Winston, you only became interested in the League of Nations when you thought it might lead to war." (Remark to Churchill.) Robert Rhodes James, *Eden,* page 204

Neville Chamberlain (1869-1940)

"The worst thing I can say about democracy is that it has tolerated the Right Honourable Gentleman for four and a half years." (Of Bevan.)

Sir Winston Churchill (1874-1965)

Churchill had a particularly low opinion of Ramsay MacDonald. "He has the gift of compressing the largest amount of words into the smallest amount of thought."

Earl of Clarendon (George William Frederick Villiers, 4th Earl of Clarendon) (1800-1870)

"The Missus". (Habitual reference to Queen Victoria which, when she discovered it, spoilt his chances of becoming Prime Minister, although she might have forgiven his occasional description of as 'Eliza'.)

Julian Critchley (1930-   )

"Mrs Thatcher requires devotion as well as obedience."
Julian Critchley, *Heseltine,* page 287

"Mrs Thatcher has hijacked the Tory Party from the land-owners and given it to the estate agents."
Today, 5 September 1989

Benjamin Disraeli, Earl of Beaconsfield (1804-1881)

"A Conservative Government is an organised hypocrisy."
17 March 1845

Walter Elliot (1888-1958)

As the coffin of George V approached Westminster Hall for the late King's lying-in-state, the Maltese Cross from it fell loose and tumbled into the gutter. The new King Edward VIII reacted with the words "Christ! What's going to happen next?" Walter Elliot was near enough to hear the King's words, and commented to Robert Boothby, "That will be the motto of the new reign".

Denis Healey (Baron Healey) (1917-   )

"Mrs Thatcher tells us she has given the French President a piece of her mind . . . not a gift I would receive with alacrity."
Today, 5 September 1989

Michael Heseltine (1933-   )

"I always knew that Neil Kinnock belonged in the economic nursery. Now, God help us, we've got twins." (Of John Smith during the run-up to the 1992 General Election.)

Neil Kinnock (1942-   )

"He's the Labour movement's nearest equivalent to a First World War general." (Of Arthur Scargill, President of the National Union of Mineworkers.)
Robert Harris, *The Making of Neil Kinnock,* page 164

"If Margaret Thatcher wins on Thursday, I warn you not to be ordinary, I warn you not to be young. I warn you not to fall ill, I warn you not to get old." (In 1983.)
Robert Harris, *The Making of Neil Kinnock,* page 208

"*The Times* is the *Sun* with long words."
Michael Leapman, *Kinnock,* page 139

Andrew Bonar Law (1858-1923)

"If I am a great man, then a good many of the great men of history are frauds."

Ken Livingstone (1945-   )

"If I blew my nose the *Daily Express* and the *Daily Mail* would say that I am trying to spread germ warfare."
Independent, 3 April 1992

David Lloyd George, 1st Earl Lloyd George of Dwyfor (1863-1945)

"A soft-nosed torpedo". (Of Asquith in 1916.)

"When they circumcised Lord Samuel they threw away the wrong bit."
Quoted in the *Listener,* 7 September 1978

Harold Macmillan, 1st Earl of Stockton (1894-1986)

"Life would have been easier if the counter-espionage work had been less effective." (Of the Vassall spy case.)
Alistair Horne, *Macmillan,* Volume II, page 469

John Major (1943-   )

"They seem to have moved from total opposition to total subservience." (Comment made on Labour's attitude to Europe during the run-up to the 1992 election.)

SALLY TOWNSEND

Lord Melbourne (William Lamb, 1st Viscount Melbourne) (1779-1848)

"English physicians kill you, the French let you die."
Stanley Weintraub, *Victoria,* page 298

John Stuart Mill (1806-1873)

"Conservatives are not necessarily stupid, but most stupid people are Conservatives." (In 1866.)

Sir Gerald Nabarro (1913-1973)

"Traditionally Tory leaders were said to 'emerge'. That is to say, the succession was rigged by a small section of the party, usually with Cabinet inspiration."
Nab: Portrait of a Politician, page 29

Lord Northcliffe (Alfred Harmsworth, 1st Viscount Northcliffe) (1865-1922)

On hearing that Lord Kitchener had been drowned, Northcliffe exclaimed, "Providence is on the side of the British Empire after all".
A.J.P. Taylor, *English History, 1914-45*

Lord Palmerston (Henry Temple, 3rd Viscount Palmerston) (1784-1865)

When Lord Palmerston heard of an exceptionally dull Scottish peer who desperately coveted an honour, Palmerston remarked, "Give him the [Order of the] Thistle; he is such an ass he is sure to eat it."
Clive Bigham, *The Prime Ministers of Britain*, page 198

Sir Robert Peel (1788-1850)

"My belief is, from all that I have seen of the French people and their Government, that they are much more likely to presume upon our weakness than to take offence at our strength."
Norman Gash, *Sir Robert Peel*, page 68

Lord Rosebery (Archibald Primrose, 5th Earl of Rosebery) (1847-1929)

"Lloyd George is a one-eyed fellow in blinkers."

"Lord Randolph Churchill was the chief mourner at his own protracted funeral."
Lord Randolph Churchill, page 181

Richard Brinsley Sheridan (1751-1816)

In reply to a political opponent, Sheridan said, "The Right Honourable Gentleman is indebted to his memory for his jests and to his imagination for his facts."

F.E. Smith, 1st Earl of Birkenhead (1872-1930)

Judge Willis: "You are offensive, sir."

F.E.S.: "We both are; the difference is that I am trying to be and you can't help it."

2nd Earl of Birkenhead, *Lord Birkenhead,* page 115

During a particularly acrimonious exchange in court Judge Willis pertly asked Lord Birkenhead, "What do you suppose I am on the bench for?"

Birkenhead replied: "It is not for me to attempt to fathom the inscrutable workings of Providence."

2nd Earl of Birkenhead, *Lord Birkenhead*

"Sir Austen Chamberlain always played the game and always lost it."

Sir David Steel (1938-   )

"I like good food and decent wine as much as Roy Jenkins does, but I keep quiet about it."

Alan Watkins, *Brief Lives,* page 173

Margaret Thatcher, Baroness Thatcher of Kesteven (1925-   )

"I can trust my husband not to fall asleep on a public platform and he usually claps in the right places."
20 August 1978

"I don't mind how much my ministers talk as long as they do what I say."
Observer, 27 January 1980

At an apocryphal banquet with the rest of her Cabinet Mrs Thatcher chose what she would like to eat.   "Vegetables?" enquired the waiter.   "Oh," said Mrs Thatcher, looking at her assembled Government, "They'll have the same."

J.H. Thomas (1874-1949)

"You've sold us," a dissatisfied NUR representative called out at a conference.
"I've tried to but I couldn't get a bid," replied Thomas.

Jeremy Thorpe (1929-   )

"The right wing of the Conservative Party is one of the most vicious, prejudiced and neolithic animals in British politics."
Sunday Telegraph, 21 April 1988

Eric Varley (1932-   )

"Putting Norman Tebbit in charge of industrial relations is like appointing Dracula to take charge of the blood transfusion service."
Today, 5 September 1989

Duke of Wellington (Arthur Wellesley, 1st Duke of Wellington (1769-1852)

"Oh, he is a very good bridge for the rats to cross over." (On hearing that William Huskisson* would join the government.)
Lord Holland, *Diary*, 8 March 1828

Lord Westbury (Richard Bethell, 1st Baron Westbury) (1800-1873)

"Turn it over once more in what you are pleased to call your mind." (In court, when a barrister stated he was turning over a question in his mind.)

* In 1830, William Huskisson became the first man to die in a railway accident when he was struck by a locomotive during the opening of the Liverpool and Manchester Railway. Ironically, he was crossing the track in order to greet the Duke of Wellington.

Harold Wilson, Baron Wilson of Rievaulx (1916-   )

"The idea I was seeking to get across was that Ulster was always ready to come to Auntie [i.e. the British Government] for spending money, expressing their thanks by kicking her in the teeth."
Final Term, page 77

"I have always said about Tony [Benn] that he immatures with age."

"Tories never actually talk about getting rid of their leader, then suddenly there is a flash of steel between the shoulder-blades and rigor mortis sets in."

CHAPTER TWO

Gentle Jibe

Contrary to popular opinion, not all political exchange is knockabout stuff. Many politicians find to their surprise that wry humour, even turned against themselves, is just as effective. Tell your opponent across the floor of the House that you agree with him, and see him covered in confusion; flattered that at least someone thinks he is right, and alarmed that his credibility with his own side will be undermined. Balfour's comment on Gladstone falls into this category; F.E. Smith pays Churchill a complex compliment which must have left the great man both puzzled and preening. Lord Derby's dismissive remark to Charles Lever on the Governorship of Trieste harks back to Sir Thomas More's sigh to Richard Rich, his betrayer: "For Wales, Sir Richard, for Wales?"* Herein lies the stuff of the most elegant insult.

The best jibes are both simple and true. Little minds in little worlds abound in politics, as Michael Foot observes. Defending their own small patch can take the place of the national interest — which is what we all thought our Members of Parliament were elected to promote — and who better to make that point than the splendid David Amess, MP, so strongly identified with Basildon since his election there in 1983?

---

* Rich's perjury ensured More's conviction and subsequent execution for treason in 1535. Rich was rewarded with the Secretaryship of Wales, which prompted More to remark to him that he could understand a man selling his soul for the world, but . . .

David Amess (1952-   )

"Honourable Members were keen to have more trains so long as the new lines did not run through their constituencies."
19 December 1990

Jack Ashley (1922-   )

Looking at the large number of ex-Ministers after the Thatcher years, Mr Ashley observed that "One of the interesting aspects of the House of Commons is the rejuvenation of members when they leave office."
19 December 1990

Herbert Henry Asquith, 1st Earl of Oxford and Asquith (1852-1928)

"The number of people who really think in any age and country is very limited, and still smaller is the number of those who think for themselves." (In 1918.)

Nancy, Lady Astor (1879-1964)

"I am the kind of woman I would run away from."

"The only thing I like about rich people is their money."

Stanley Baldwin, 1st Earl Baldwin of Bewdley (1867-1947)

Stanley Baldwin was supposedly a very easy-going man. Once he was asked if he didn't sometimes enjoy a good fight. "Oh yes," he replied, "I like the other man to begin the fight and then I am ready."

Trying to rouse Stanley Baldwin, it was pointed out to him that Lloyd George was a very forceful personality, capable of battering down all opposition. Baldwin agreed: "A dynamic force is a very terrible thing. It may crush you, but it is not necessarily right."

Baldwin finally became an Earl and, looking round him ruefully, observed that "There is perhaps a certain retributive justice in it as I have sent so many others here, hoping I should never see their faces again."
William Douglas-Home, *The Prime Minister,* page 205

A.J. Balfour, 1st Earl of Balfour (1848-1930)

It was once put to Balfour that although Leader of the Liberals, Gladstone was actually a Tory. "Yes," Balfour mused, "Gladstone was a Tory in everything but essentials."

"I thought he was a young man of promise; but it appears he was a young man of promises." (Of Winston Churchill in 1899.)
Randolph S. Churchill, *Winston Churchill,* Volume I, page 449

Anthony Wedgwood Benn (1925-   )

"Harold [Wilson] rejected my proposal for a programme on world poverty on TV on the eve of the municipal elections."
Diary, 23 March 1964

"It is obvious that I shall have to abandon my hopes of getting the Queen's head off the stamps."
Diary, 31 December 1965

"Middle-class Labour leaders are recaptured by the Establishment when they die."
Diary, 7 November 1967

"There is the No-Turning-Back-Group — I believe that was the battle cry of the Gadarene Swine."

Humphry Berkeley (1926-   )

"The main difference between Churchill and Powell is that Churchill did not have any desire to be martyred."
The Odyssey of Enoch: A Political Memoir, page 709

Edmund Burke (1729-1797)

"It is a general popular error to suppose the loudest complainers for the public to be the most anxious for its welfare."

Barbara Castle, Baroness Castle of Blackburn, (1911-   )

"The row of pegs was always filled with her clothes." (Of Mrs Thatcher).
Hugo Young, *One of Us,* page 307

Sir (Alfred) Duff Cooper, 1st Viscount Norwich (1890-1954)

"One can make a joke but one can't be one."
John Chambers, *Duff Cooper,* page 233

Lord Derby (Edward Stanley, 14th Earl of Derby-) (1799-1869)

Lord Derby had a great ability to combine compliments and insults. In 1867, he awarded the Governorship of Trieste to Charles Lever, telling him, "Here is £600 a year for doing nothing, and you are just the man to do it."

Sir Anthony Eden, 1st Earl of Avon (1897-1977)

"It is a common happening that those in power, as their tenure of office continues, find themselves less and less able to contemplate relinquishing it."

"And he's sensible in spite of that." (On being told that Sir Roger Making had taken a brilliant First at Oxford.)
Lord Moran, *Struggle for Survival,* page 376

Michael Foot (1913-   )

"Politicians live in little worlds of their own and imagine these are the universe."
Another Heart, page 33

Edward Gibbon (1737-1794)

"When the promise of eternal happiness was proposed to mankind on condition of adopting the faith and of observing the precepts of the Gospels, it is no wonder that so advantageous an offer should have been accepted by great numbers of every religion, of every rank and of every province in the Roman Empire."
The Decline and Fall of the Roman Empire, Chapter VI

W.E. Gladstone (1809-1898)

"Liberalism is trust of the people tempered by prudence. Conservatism is distrust of the people tempered by fear."

Lord Hailsham (Quintin Hogg, Baron Hailsham of St Marylebone) (1907-   )

"The real price one pays for a lay magistracy is, of course, undue lenience."

Marquess of Halifax (George Savile, 1st Marquess of Halifax) (1633-1695)

"The best Party is but a kind of conspiracy against the nation."

"If men would think more, they would act less."

"They who are of the opinion that money will do everything may well be suspected to do everything for money."

"When it is said of a man 'he knows how to live', it may be implied he is not very honest."

Denis Healey, Baron Healey (1917-   )

"Nothing is more dangerous than the politician who uses politics as a surrogate for an unsatisfactory personal life."
The Time of my Life, page 564

Sir Edward Heath (1916-   )

"If politicians lived on praise and thanks, they'd be forced into some other line of business."

"I do not often attack the Labour Party, they do it so well themselves."

"I don't think modesty is the outstanding characteristic of contemporary politics, do you?" (In 1988.)

Sidney Herbert, 1st Baron Herbert of Lea (1810-1861)

Shortly before he died, Sidney Herbert was given a peerage. A friend asked him if he found talking in the House of Lords difficult. "Difficult?" he replied. "It was like addressing sheeted tombstones by moonlight."
Cecil Woodham-Smith, *Florence Nightingale,* page 358

Roy Jenkins, Baron Jenkins of Hillhead (1920-   )

"According to which way you look at it, Mr Heath has stubbornness or determination."
John Campbell, *Roy Jenkins,* page 155

Robert Kilroy-Silk (1942-   )

"Things must be getting really bad. Denis Healey stopped me at the Members' Entrance tonight. 'Hello Bob,' he said warmly."
Hard Labour, page 131

Lord Liverpool (Robert Jenkinson, 2nd Earl of Liverpool) (1770-1828)

"If we could do what we *ought* to do (Do not be alarmed, I am not going to propose it)."
Norman Gash, *Lord Liverpool,* page 219

David Lloyd George, 1st Earl Lloyd George of Dwyfor (1863-1945)

"Poor Bonar [Law] can't bear being called a liar. Now I don't mind."

Robert Lowe, Viscount Sherbrooke (1811-1892)

"Here lies the body of Robert Lowe
Where he's gone to, I don't know.
If he's gone to realms above,
There's an end to peace and love,
If he sought a lower level,
God have mercy on the Devil."
(Anonymous — suggested epitaph.)

"I believe it will be absolutely necessary that you should prevail on our future masters to learn their letters." (On the middle classes being given the vote in 1867. Often misquoted as "we must educate our masters".)
15 July 1867

James Ramsay MacDonald (1866-1937)

MacDonald: "Now mark my words, that Professor Lindbergh is no good at all."

Harold Nicolson: "Lindemann?"

MacDonald: "Of course, of course I meant Linderbergh."*

Harold Macmillan, 1st Earl of Stockton (1894-1986)

"As usual, the Liberals offer a mixture of sound and original ideas. Unfortunately none of the sound ideas is original, and none of the original ideas is sound."
Observer, 1961

Lord Mancroft (Stormont Mancroft, 2nd Baron) (1914-1987)

"The only exercise I ever take is walking up hospital stairs to visit friends who've damaged themselves by taking exercise."
A Chinaman in my Bath

"There are only three things to learn from skiing: how to put on your skis, how to slide downhill, and how to walk along the hospital corridor."
A Chinaman in my Bath

---

*Professor Lindemann (later 1st Viscount Cherwell) was a noted scientist, a friend and adviser to Churchill, an expert on aerodynamics, a professor of philosophy at Oxford and, during the Second World War, a scientific adviser to the Cabinet. Charles Lindbergh became the first man to fly the Atlantic solo in 1927.

Ian Mikardo (1908-   )

"We've elevated self-interest into virtue."
Back Bencher, page 219

Field-Marshal Viscount Montgomery of Alamein (1887-1976)

"I've spent my life fighting the Germans and fighting the politicians. It is much easier to fight the Germans."

"Anyone who votes Labour ought to be locked up."   (While campaigning for Churchill in Woodford in 1959.)

Lord Moran (Charles Wilson, 1st Baron Moran) (1882-1977)

"When Churchill spoke of miners it seemed to put the next General Election into his head."
Struggle for Survival, page 349

Herbert Morrison, Baron Morrison of Lambeth (1888-1965)

"There is a difference between intellectuals who rise with the Labour movement and those who rise on it."
B. Donaghue and G.W. Jones, *Herbert Morrison,* page 340

David Penhaligon (1944-1986)

"Who could be luckier than to be paid fairly well, which to be honest MPs are, for pursuing their hobby? That's what politics is."

Annette Penhaligon, *Penhaligon*, page 229

"I have always realised that I only got elected because I was too naive to realise it was impossible."

Annette Penhaligon, *Penhaligon*, page 1

William Pitt (the Elder), 1st Earl of Chatham (1708-1778)

"The atrocious crime of being a young man I shall neither attempt to palliate nor deny."

29 January 1741

Enoch Powell (1912-   )

"If in the words which the Secretary of State has just used, the use of a nuclear weapon is to be avoided 'at all costs', what is the point of having one?"

24 January 1984

James Prior, Baron Prior of Brampton (1927-   )

"I do not regard the swing to 'Thatcherism' — as it has been called — as more than a passing phenomenon in the evolution of the Conservative Party."

A Balance of Power, page 261

Lord Reith (John Reith, 1st Baron Reith of Stonehaven) (1889-1971)

Lord Reith was once asked if the Government's planning policy still stood, to which he gave the celebrated reply, "The Government's planning policy still stands and is standing still."
Roger Milne, *Reith,* page 271

Nicholas Ridley, Baron Ridley of Liddesdale (1929-   )

"Normal humdrum government has been resumed." (On the fall of Mrs Thatcher.)
My Style of Government, page 267

Bertrand Russell, 3rd Earl Russell (1872-1970)

"It is the failure to take oneself less seriously which marks immaturity."
Barry Feinberg and Ronald Kasrils, *Dear Bertrand Russell,* page 11

Lord Salisbury (Robert Cecil, 3rd Marquess of Salisbury) (1830-1903)

"By office boys for office boys." (Description of the *Daily Mail.*)

"Lord Salisbury, who owned a villa on the Riviera, said the neighbourhood had two drawbacks, 'Flies in summer, Royalties in winter'."

Emmanuel Shinwell, Baron Shinwell (1884-1986)

"We are legislating for common people, some of them very common people, and we ought to use language that is really understood by them."
30 March 1938

F.E. Smith, 1st Earl of Birkenhead (1872-1930)

"Churchill is easily satisfied with the best."
Sir John Colville, *The Churchills*, page 215

Philip Snowden, 1st Viscount Snowden (1864-1937)

"For your private information, I may say that my ideal cabinet would be one in which I held all the offices."

Harold Wilson, Baron Wilson of Rievaulx (1916-   )

"One of the oddities of the politics of 1970 was the cooling-down of the issue of law and order from the day that the Conservatives came back to power."
The Labour Government, 1964-70

"My last official engagement was the Monday Cabinet — a Budget Cabinet. Denis Healey outlined his proposals in some detail. He was going to increase the tax on cigarettes, but not pipe-tobacco, which he explained was much consumed by retired persons."
Michael Korda, *Power in the Office*, page 239

"There is a famous story about a Welsh fifteen at Cardiff Arms Park. For twenty minutes, ankle-deep in mud, the forwards hardly released the ball from the scrum for a moment. At last it emerged to the scrum-half who passed to the fly-half, who then kicked it high over the grandstand. A search party set off to look for it, and after ten minutes had not returned. One of the Welsh pack — or it may have been the English — was heard to say, "Never mind the ruddy ball, let's get on with the ruddy game".
7 December 1974

Woodrow Wyatt, Baron Wyatt of Weeford (1918-   )

"In politics some deceit or moral dishonesty is the oil without which the machinery would not work."
Sunday Times, 1973

CHAPTER THREE

Sexism Rules, OK?

Of course there's sex in politics — and sexism too, however officiously pedants may strive to ensure we use only "politically correct" language. If that means offending no one, the objective may be laudable, but the result would be a far duller world.

Most of the women in British politics, both today and in the past, seem perfectly capable of taking care of themselves. Lady Astor, an American, was the first woman to sit in the House of Commons, winning a by-election in her husband's place in 1919 when he succeeded to the House of Lords. She became known for her repartee on the stump. Challenged by a farmworker as to her knowledge of rural affairs, she demanded that he put a question to her.

"Well then, how many toes has a pig got?" he asked. "You take off your boot, my man, and count them," was her riposte.

This lady could look after herself. The reply she made, after an exchange about temperance at a different meeting is not, however, recorded (she was a lifelong campaigner against alcohol after an unhappy first marriage which ended in divorce). Waving a bottle of whisky over her head, she told her audience, "I would rather commit adultery than touch a drop of this stuff!" and glared at them. "Well, who wouldn't?" came the rejoinder.

Nancy, Lady Astor (1879-1964)

Field-Marshal Montgomery once unwisely told Lady Astor that he did not approve of women politicians. "Oh, that's all right," she replied, "The only General I approve of is Evangeline Booth."*

Although herself one to ridicule people who said uninteresting things, she once assured a rapt House "Between the ages of fifteen and twenty, boys become men and girls become women", adding a little later, for good measure, "So far as sex goes it is as important for boys as it is for girls".

Stanley Baldwin, 1st Earl Baldwin of Bewdley (1867-1947)

"But did he spend the nights at home? (On being told that Charles II went to church every day during Lent.)

A.J. Balfour, 1st Earl of Balfour (1848-1930)

On being asked whether he would marry Margot Tennant (who later married Asquith), Balfour replied, "No, I rather think of having a career of my own."

*Daughter of 'General' William Booth, the founder of the Salvation Army.

Anthony Wedgwood Benn (1925-   )

"Having served in eleven Parliaments, it would be difficult to describe this as a maiden speech. It would be like Elizabeth Taylor appearing at her next wedding in a white gown."
6 March 1984

"Anyone who wants to see real division in society should go to the House of Lords, where the lavatories differentiate between peeresses and ladies."
Independent, 7 March 1992

Lord Boothby (Robert, Baron Boothby) (1900-1986)

Once, during an *Any Questions* programme, Boothby was asked what he would do if he woke up and found that he had changed sex. "Go for a walk and see what happened," he replied.

Fenner Brockway, Baron Brockway (1888-1988)

"'Let him who is without sin be the first to accuse'. No humiliation of the woman; her accusers hurrying away ashamed. Perfect."
Towards Tomorrow, page 266

Lord Byron (George Gordon Noel Byron, 6th Baron) (1788-1824)

"Maidens, like moths, are ever caught by glare
And Mammon wins his way where seraphs might despair."
Childe Harold's Pilgrimage, Canto I, stanza 9

Barbara Castle, Baroness Castle of Blackburn (1911-   )

"If she would only occasionally come in with a smut on her nose, her hair dishevelled, looking as if she'd been wrestling with her soul, as I do." (Of Margaret Thatcher.)
Hugo Young, *One of Us*, page 122

On Margaret Thatcher becoming Tory leader: "She is so clearly the best man among them."
The Castle Diaries 1974-76, entry for 11 February 1975

"I have never consciously exploited the fact that I am a woman. I wouldn't dare try that even if I knew how to. I have too much respect for my male colleagues to think they would be particularly impressed."
Interview with Kenneth Harris, 5 October 1969

Lord Chesterfield (Philip Stanhope, 4th Earl of Chesterfield) (1694-1773)

Writing to his illegitimate son about sex: "The pleasure is momentary; the position ridiculous; and the expense damnable."

Sir Winston Churchill (1874-1965)

During the Second World War it was reported to Churchill that a retired admiral had been caught with a call-girl in St James's Park early one winter's morning.

"Now," said Churchill, "Let's get this straight. Are you saying he was actually with a young girl at 6am in the morning with frost on the grass? And that he was seventy-five?" The report was confirmed as correct.

"By God," chortled the Prime Minister, "Makes one proud to be British."

Earl of Clarendon (George William Frederick Villiers, 4th Earl of Clarendon) (1800-1870)

"Pray burn this letter directly, like a good woman as you are." (To the Duchess of Manchester, and found stowed among her effects.)

Edwina Currie (1946-   )

On being asked in 1987 by businessmen for advice about precautions against catching AIDS abroad: "Take the wife. Failing that, take a good book."

"The Labour Party is being led by a woman; she has never stood for election and is leading the Labour Party by the nose. She's the woman who makes the breakfast in the Kinnock household." (On Neil and Glenys Kinnock, 1987.)

Lord Curzon (George Nathaniel Curzon, 1st Marquess Curzon of Kedleston) (1859-1925)

"Better send them a Papal Bull." (Comment about a printing error in a Foreign Office document, which read "the monks of Mount Athos were violating their cows".)

Hugh Dalton, Baron Dalton (1887-1962)

After an air raid Dalton telephoned his wife. "Is that you, Ruth? A terrible raid. I suddenly remembered that I had left my new suit in the flat. It would be a nuisance if that blew up."

Benjamin Disraeli, Earl of Beaconsfield (1804-1881)

"Lady Lytton rules her husband, but that I suppose is always the case where marriages are what is called 'happy'."

After a dinner at the home of a society hostess: "If only the food had been as warm as the champagne, and the champagne as cold as her heart!"

"I wanted a reason, and you gave me an excuse." (On being told that a couple were getting married because they loved each other.)

Marcia Falkender, Baroness Falkender (1932-   )

"The majority of women politicians are intelligent. It takes a special sort of man to like the company of intelligent women, and a very special sort of male politician to like the company of intelligent female politicians."
Downing Street in Perspective

Lord Gladwyn (Hubert Gladwyn Jebb, 1st Baron) (1900-   )

"The Commissar's Club at Kalinin
Is the best club that I've ever been in.
Said a chap from Odessa,
'You watch me undress her',
As he brought a young girl of thirteen in."
Hugh Dalton, *War Diary*, page 334

Jo Grimond, Baron Grimond (1913-   )

"I have long believed that women should play a much bigger part in our affairs."
Memoirs, page 285

Lord Halifax (Edward Wood, 1st Earl of Halifax) (1881-1959)

"Lord Halifax recently heard the word 'pansy' and had to send for one of his secretaries to ask the meaning of the word."
Robert Rhodes James (ed.), *Chips: The Diaries of Sir Henry Channon*, 1934 entry

Sir Edward Heath (1916-   )

"Pitt saved Europe from Napoleon, he was the pilot who weathered the storm. I don't know whether he'd have done it any better or quicker had he been married." (On being a bachelor.)

"A man who got married in order to be a better Prime Minister wouldn't be either a good Prime Minister or a good husband."
Margaret Laing, *Heath*, page 179

A.P. Herbert (Sir Alan Herbert) (1890-1971)

On marriage: "Holy Deadlock".

Lord Kitchener (Field-Marshal Earl Kitchener of Khartoum) (1850-1916)

"My colleagues tell military secrets to their wives, except Asquith, who tells them to other people's wives."
Philip Magnus, *Kitchener —Portrait of an Imperialist*

Joseph Lister, 1st Baron Lister (1827-1912)

"Another proposal which I could scarcely believe my eyes in reading was that all medical students of the University of Glasgow to be compelled to attend clinical teaching given to male and female students."
Richard Fisher, *Joseph Lister*, page 324

Ken Livingstone (1945-   )

"Almost everyone has the sexual potential for anything."
Citizen Ken, page 91

Selwyn Lloyd (John Selwyn Brooke Lloyd, Baron Selwyn Lloyd) (1904-1978)

"But he couldn't have had the time!" (Of the 1963 Profumo scandal.)
D.K. Thorpe, *Selwyn Lloyd*, page 439

David Lloyd George, 1st Earl Lloyd George of Dwyfor (1863-1945)

"You cannot trust the interests of any class entirely to another class; and you cannot trust the interests of any sex to another sex."
1911

Lloyd George once asked Lady Astor, "What are you doing with my secretary, Philip Kerr?" To which she replied indignantly, "Absolutely nothing."
"Then," retorted Lloyd George, "You ought to be ashamed of yourself."

Lord Longford (Francis Pakenham, 7th Earl of Longford) (1905-   )

"No sex without responsibility."
Observer, 3 May 1954

James Ramsay MacDonald (1866-1937)

"The people do not mind fornication but they loathe adultery."
(On the reign of Edward VIII, to Harold Nicolson, 13 July 1936.)

Lord Mancroft (Stormont Mancroft, 2nd Baron) (1914-1987)

"Before the war you took your secretary to Paris and called her your wife. Now, in order to wriggle through the tax-gatherers' net, you take your wife to Paris and call her your secretary."
A Chinaman in my Bath

Lord Moran (Charles Wilson, 1st Baron Moran) (1882-1977)

"Penicillin will make lust safe for democracy."
Struggle for Survival, page 191

Herbert Morrison, Baron Morrison of Lambeth (1888-1965)

"I would be tempted to pardon any man who chopped off the head of a nagging wife." (On the death penalty.)

Lord Palmerston (Henry Temple, 3rd Viscount Palmerston) (1784-1865)

When over seventy Palmerston was alleged to have committed adultery with a certain Miss O'Kane. It was remarked that the lady was certainly Kane, but was Palmerston Abel?
Ridley, *Palmerston*, page 532

Reginald Paget, Baron Paget of Northampton (1908-1990)

"What do these rumours amount to? They amount to the fact that a Minister is said to be acquainted with a particularly pretty girl. I should have thought that were a matter of congratulation rather than enquiry." (Of the Profumo affair, 21 March 1963.)

Emmeline Pankhurst (1858-1928)

On violence used to further the Suffragettes' cause: "The argument of the broken pane of glass is the most valuable argument in modern politics."
Votes for Women

Lord Queensberry (John Sholto Douglas, 8th Marquess of Queensberry) (1844-1900)

Lord Queensberry became increasingly furious concerning Oscar Wilde's fondness for Queensberry's son, Lord Alfred Douglas, known as 'Bosie'. Unable to prove the worst, Queensberry faced Wilde with the words, "I do not say that you are but I say that you look it, and that is just as bad."

James Prior, Baron Prior of Brampton (1927-   )

"It takes a strong marriage to survive a long political career."
Balance of Power, page 249

Tim Renton (1932-   )

Dennis Skinner asked Tim Renton, as Minister for the Civil Service, "How many civil servants are a) men, b) women?" To which Renton replied "All of them".
6 February 1992

Lord Rosebery (Archibald Primrose, 5th Earl of Rosebery) (1847-1929)

"Do not first announce action, and then, when you are unable to take action, withdraw, because you will only find yourself in the same position as now, plus a public and humiliating confession of impotence."

Lord John Russell (1st Earl Russell) (1792-1878)

"Two mothers-in-law."   (On being asked to suggest a suitable punishment for bigamy.)

Richard Brinsley Sheridan (1751-1816)

"'Tis safest in matrimony to begin with a little aversion."
The Rivals

Alfred, Lord Tennyson (1809-1892)

"Man is the hunter; woman is his game."
The Princess, V, line 147

"God made the woman for the man."
Edwin Morris, line 15

Margaret Thatcher, Baroness Thatcher of Kesteven (1925-   )

"I have always thought of myself as a politician who happens to be a woman."
Patrick Murray, *Margaret Thatcher*, page 208

Referring to the possibility of a woman becoming Prime Minister: "I don't think it will come in my lifetime." (To Anthony King, on 14 January 1972.)

"One of the things politics has taught me is that men are not a reasoned or reasonable sex." (To Anthony King, 14 January 1972.)

"The cocks may crow but it's the hen that lays the egg."
Denis Healey, *The Time of My Life*

"The home should be the centre but not the boundary of a woman's life."
Hugo Young, *One of Us*, page 306

Sir Denis Thatcher (1915   )

Discussing his domestic arrangements with a reporter, Denis Thatcher was asked who wore the pants in his house. "I do," he replied, "and I also wash and iron them."

Lord Thorneycroft (Peter, Baron Thorneycroft) (1909-   )

"It is important to recognise that Mrs Thatcher is a woman. They're not like us and it's no good pretending that they are." Patrick Murray, *Margaret Thatcher*, page 229

Sidney Webb, 1st Baron Passfield (1859-1947)

"Marriage is the waste-paper basket of the emotions." Bertrand Russell, *Portraits from Memory*

Lord Whitelaw (William Whitelaw, 1st Viscount) (1918-   )

"I was one of those people who was always rather frightened of women politicians." Patrick Murray, *Margaret Thatcher*, page 116

Harold Wilson, Baron Wilson of Rievaulx (1916-   )

"We discussed a title [for a White Paper]. [Barbara Castle] laid claim to Labour and Productivity. I suggested with a lady minister this might lead to bar-room ribaldry. She took the point and we settled on Employment and Productivity."
The Labour Government 1964-1970, page 521

Woodrow Wyatt, Baron Wyatt of Weeford (1918-   )

"A man falls in love through his eyes, a woman through her ears."

To the Point, 1981

CHAPTER FOUR

Wit and Wisdom

"I wish I'd said that ...." When I was young and struggling, the *Dictionary of Quotations* was the essential second stop for any debater, the first stop being the dictionary itself— hence all those school debates beginning "It depends what you mean by Sovereignty ...." How marvellous to find a dollop of insight elegantly expressed, with the authority of a famous speaker or writer thrown in for free. Using several quotations suggested erudition. Using lots eliminated entirely the need to write or say anything original whatsoever.

Churchill had it right on political skill, given the number of times ministers and — more recently — pollsters have had to explain why a racing certainty never made it to the first fence. In this chapter you will find the most convincing of excuses with which to flavour your own discourse, and thereby — with luck — leave your listeners deeply impressed and content. Me? I'd rather be quoted ....

Lord Aberdeen (George Gordon, 4th Earl of Aberdeen) (1784-1860)

"It may be true that every necessary war must also really be a just war; but it does not absolutely follow that every just war is a necessary war."
Sir Arthur Gordon, *Lord Aberdeen*, page 303

Lord Acton (John Dalberg, 1st Baron Acton) (1834-1902)

"Power tends to corrupt and absolute power corrupts absolutely."
1887

"The most certain test by which we judge whether a country is really free is the amount of security enjoyed by its minorities."
1877

Clement Attlee, 1st Earl Attlee (1883-1967)

When Attlee was eighty, a reporter asked him what he felt like. "Better than the alternative," was his clipped reply.

Someone once told Attlee that the House of Commons was terribly overcrowded. Without a flicker of a smile he replied: "Whenever I have been here, there has been a very scanty attendance."

When Herbert Morrison had finished his autobiography Attlee was asked whether it made an interesting story. "Yes," he replied, "a fine work of fiction."

"Few thought he was even a starter,
There were many who thought themselves smarter.
But he ended PM,
CH and OM,*
An Earl and a Knight of the Garter."
(On himself.)

"Russian Communism is the illegitimate child of Karl Marx and Catherine the Great."
Observer, 1956

Attlee summed up his attitude towards liberty fairly succinctly: "The real test of one's belief in the doctrine of Habeas Corpus is not when one demands its application on behalf of one's friends, but of one's enemies."
Kenneth Harris, *Attlee*, page 228

"The only alternative to coexistence is co-death."

Sir Francis Bacon, Viscount St Alban (1561-1626)

"If a man will begin with certainties he shall end in doubts, but if he will be content to begin with doubts, he shall end in certainties."
Advancement of Learning, I, v, 8

*Respectively, Prime Minister, Companion of Honour, and Order of Merit.

"Hope is a good breakfast, but it is a bad supper."
Apothegms, 36

"To spend too much time in studies is sloth."
Essays, 'Of Studies'

"A wise man will make more opportunities than he finds."
Essays, 'Of Ceremonies and Respects'

"In government change is suspected, though to the better."
Filum Labyrinthi

"It is a strange desire, to seek power and to lose liberty."
Essays, 'Of Great Place'

"It is hard in all causes, but especially in religion, when voices shall be numbered and not weighed."
Essays, 'Of Church Controversies'

**Lord Baden-Powell (Robert Baden-Powell, 1st Baron)
(1857-1941)**

"Life is only a temporary affair, after all."
Tim Jeal, *Baden-Powell,* page 519

Stanley Baldwin, 1st Earl Baldwin of Bewdley (1867-1947)

"When I was a little boy in Worcestershire reading history books I never thought I should have to interfere between a king and his mistress." (Of the Abdication Crisis.)

A.J. Balfour, 1st Earl of Balfour (1848-1930)

"Biography should be written by an acute enemy."
Observer, 30 January 1929

"Nothing matters very much and very few things matter at all."

"Yes." (On being asked which of two courses should be adopted.)
Piers Brendon, *Eminent Victorians,* page 115

"What a pity." (On being assured that New York's latest skyscrapers were fireproof.)
Piers Brendon, *Eminent Victorians,* page 119

Lord Beaverbrook (William Maxwell Aitken, 1st Baron Beaverbrook) (1879-1964)

"'The right to work' is a slogan which should be accepted by every democracy."

Beaverbrook was once asked what the Common Market really meant for Britain. Could he give a brief reply in, say, a couple of words? "Yes," he replied, "Political subjection."

Ernest Bevin (1881-1951)

"What astounds me about the history of the British Navy is how cheaply we have policed the world for 300 years."
Hansard, 7 November 1945

"Civilisation cannot survive if it rests on a propertyless proletariat." (To the Transport and General Workers' Union.)
18 August 1941

John Bright (1811-1889)

"Force is not a remedy."
Birmingham, 16 November 1880

Fenner Brockway, Baron Brockway (1888-1988)

"There is some truth in the saying that we can love humanity and be less than considerate to individuals."
Towards Tomorrow, page 262

Lord Brougham (Henry Brougham, 1st Baron Brougham and Vaux) (1778-1868)

"Education makes a people easy to lead but difficult to drive; easy to govern but impossible to enslave."

Edmund Burke (1729-1797)

"Government is a contrivance of human wisdom to provide for human wants."

Lord Chesterfield (Philip Stanhope, 4th Earl of Chesterfield) (1694-1773)

"An injury is much sooner forgotten than an insult."
9 October 1746

Sir Winston Churchill (1874-1965)

When he was a young reporter Churchill also wanted to go on active service, reminding his superiors that "It is better to be making the news than taking it."

"Political skill is the ability to foretell what is going to happen ... and to have the ability afterwards to explain why it did not happen."

During the First World War Churchill described the outcome of a quarrel between the Admiralty and the Treasury about the number of battleships that should be built. "The Admiralty has demanded six, the Treasury said we could only afford four, so we finally compromised on eight."

"A good party man puts his party above himself and his country above his party."

When he was at school he was reluctant to study Classics. It was impressed upon him that Gladstone read Homer for fun. "Serves him right," retorted the young Winston.
My Early Life

Earl of Clarendon (George William Frederick Villiers, 4th Earl of Clarendon) (1800-1870)

On the popularity of Disraeli: "A Conservative is a man who turns round and round so often he becomes Dizzy." (To the Duchess of Manchester.)
2 November 1868

Richard Crossman (1907-1974)

"Where you live matters terribly."
Anthony Howard (ed.), *The Crossman Diaries*, page 237

Edwina Currie (1946-   )

"One man's priority is another man's extravagance."

Hugh Dalton (Baron Dalton) (1887-1962)

"You can't have a motion without a debate." (On his deathbed, when a nurse told him he should stop arguing and have an enema.)

Lord Denning (Alfred, Baron Denning) (1899-   )

"The Chaplain looks at the assembled members — with their varied intelligence — and then prays for the country." (On House of Commons Prayers.)
Family Star, page 185

"Jack of all trades and Master of one." (When Master of the Rolls.)
Family Star, page 204

Lord Derby (Edward Stanley, 14th Earl of Derby) (1799-1869)

A vintner once told Lord Derby that he could cure his gout with a special brand of sherry. Bearing in mind that Derby was about to resign the Premiership owing to gout, the salesman had high hopes of concluding a deal. He was disappointed with the reply, "I have tasted your sherry and prefer my gout."

Benjamin Disraeli, Earl of Beaconsfield (1804-1881)

"Nature has given us two ears but only one mouth."
Henrietta Temple, Book IV, Chapter 24

"It is much easier to be critical than correct."
24 January 1860

"My idea of an agreeable person is a person who agrees with me."
Hugo Bohun, Chapter 41

"No Government can be long secure without a formidable opposition."
Coningsby, Book II, Chapter 1

"There is moderation even in excess."
Vivian Grey, Book VI, Chapter 1

Sir Anthony Eden, 1st Earl of Avon (1897-1977)

During a lengthy Cabinet discussion about the economy, Eden looked up at his colleagues and wearily observed: "Everybody is always in favour of general economy and particular expenditure."

"The more the planners, the worse the plans."

Walter Elliot (1888-1958)

"If the tide is running with you, you can do no wrong, and if it is running against you, you can do no right."
Andrew Roberts, *The Holy Fox: A Biography of Lord Halifax*, page 268

Hugh Gaitskell (1906-1963)

"We really must keep under control, and pretty strict control, the area within which 'The Man in Whitehall' knows best."
1956

Edward Gibbon (1737-1794)

"The theologian may indulge the pleasing task of describing Religion as she descended from Heaven, arrayed in her native purity. A more melancholy duty is imposed on the historian."
The Decline and Fall of the Roman Empire, Chapter XI

Sir Ian Gilmour (1926-   )

"Monetarism is the uncontrollable in pursuit of the indefensible."
1981

W.E. Gladstone (1809-1898)

"A very fair Cabinet today — only three resignations."
S.H. Jeyes, *Lord Rosebery,* page 61

"All the world over, I will back the masses against the classes."
28 June 1886

Sir Edward Grey, 1st Viscount Grey of Fallodon (1862-1933)

"Two temptations that impair the value of their work inevitably beset public men who write memoirs. One is a tendency to reconstruct the past to suit the present views and feelings of the writer; the other is a natural desire to set his own part in affairs in a pleasing light."
Twenty-Five Years, Volume I, Page 25

Lord Hailsham (Quintin Hogg, Baron Hailsham of St Marylebone) (1907-   )

"The public will get the kind of public men it deserves."

"They said 'We want a Labour Government and we want Winston to be Prime Minister'. That's what they said to me when I was canvassing.

"I said 'Well, you can't have that, you have got to choose', and they said 'Isn't it a free country? We can vote for what we like." (Of the 1945 General Election.)
Martin Gilbert, *Churchill*, BBC1, January 1992

Marquess of Halifax (George Savile, 1st Marquess of Halifax) (1633-1695)

"When the people contend for their liberty they seldom get anything by their victory except new masters."

A.P. Herbert (Sir Alan Herbert) (1890-1971)

"The Common Law of England has been laboriously built upon a mythical figure — the figure of 'The Reasonable Man'."

"An Act of God was defined as something which no reasonable man could have expected."

Michael Heseltine (1933-   )

"They say a man should be judged by his enemies. I am very proud of mine."
April 1990

"I am humble enough to recognise that I have made mistakes, but politically astute enough to know that I have forgotten what they are."
Daily Telegraph, 4 April 1992

Sir Geoffrey Howe, Baron Howe of Aberavon (1926-   )

Sir Geoffrey Howe (as he then was) once lost his trousers on a train, and was told by a colleague, "I was thrilled about the loss of your trousers because it revealed your human face."
Observer, 12 January 1984

Neil Kinnock (1942-   )

"Two negatives don't make a positive, any more than two half-wits make a wit."

James William Lowther, 1st Viscount Ullswater (1855-1949)

"There are three golden rules for Parliamentary speakers, 'Stand up, speak up, shut up'."
1919

Lord Macaulay (Thomas Babington Macaulay, 1st Baron) (1800-1859)

"An acre in Middlesex is better than a principality in Utopia."
Essay on Lord Bacon

James Ramsay MacDonald (1866-1937)

"How can a body be selected with the power to declare a threat of world peace?" (On the League of Nations.)

Harold Mackintosh, 1st Viscount Mackintosh of Halifax (1891-1964)

"If we can't save sinners then let's make sinners save." (On the introduction of Premium Bonds.)

Iain Macleod (1913-1970)

"History is too serious to be left to historians."
Observer, 16 July 1961

John Major (1943-   )

"Some people eat eggs, I wear them." (Referring to an incident during the 1992 election campaign when an egg, thrown by a demonstrator, had splattered his suit.)

"I can't legislate to change human nature."
Observer, 21 June 1992

Lord Melbourne (William Lamb, 1st Viscount Melbourne) (1779-1848)

"What the wise men promised hasn't happened and what all the damned fools said would happen, has happened." (On Catholic emancipation. 1829.)
H. Dunckley, *Melbourne*

"Be not over solicitous about education. It may be able to do much, but it does not do as much as expected from it. It may mould and direct the character, but it rarely alters it."
1 December 1841

John Morley, 1st Viscount Morley of Blackburn (1838-1923)

"Those who would treat politics and morality apart will never understand the one or the other."
Life of Rousseau, page 380

"The proper memory for a politician is one that knows what to remember and what to forget."
Recollection, Volume II

Sir Robert Peel (1788-1850)

"The real truth is, the number of convicts is too overwhelming for the means of proper and effectual punishment. I despair of any remedy but that which I wish I could hope for — a great reduction in the amount of crime."
Norman Gash, *Sir Robert Peel*, page 68

Mr Speaker Popham (Sir John Popham) (1531?-1607)

When John Major made a speech in the House of Commons welcoming the election of Miss Betty Boothroyd as Speaker, he referred to a previous Speaker of the House: "When Mr Popham was Speaker in 1581, and the Lower House had sat long, and done, in effect, nothing, coming one day to Queen Elizabeth, she said to him: 'Now, Mr Speaker, what hath passed in the Lower House?" He answered: "If it please Your Majesty, seven weeks.' "
27 April 1992

Sir Robert Rhodes James (1933-   )

"It often happens that people come to believe in their own fictions."
Anthony Eden, page 458

"One of the most important factors in life, politics and war, to which historians tend to devote too little attention, is sheer luck, good or ill."
Anthony Eden, page 428

"Justice in politics has an uncomfortable habit of being rough."
Anthony Eden, page 586

Bertrand Russell, 3rd Earl Russell (1872-1970)

"Every sane and sensible and quiet thing we do is absolutely ignored by the Press."
Face to Face, BBC TV, 1959

Lord Salisbury (Robert Cecil, 3rd Marquess of Salisbury) (1830-1903)

"If you believe the doctors, nothing is wholesome; if you believe the theologians, nothing is innocent; if you believe the soldiers, nothing is safe."
Letter to Lord Lytton, 15 June 1877

"Industry cannot flow unless capital is confident, and capital will not be confident as long as it fears that Parliament will meddle with it and walk off with its profits."
Robert Taylor, *Salisbury*, page 86

"It is one of the misfortunes of our political system that parties are formed more with reference to controversies that are gone by than to the controversies which these parties have actually to decide."
Quarterly Review, January 1866

Lord Sidmouth (Henry Addington, 1st Viscount Sidmouth) (1757-1844)

"In youth, the absence of pleasure is pain, in old age, the absence of pain is pleasure."

Sir Cyril Smith (1928-   )

"Parliament is the longest-running farce in the West End."

Lord Soper (The Rev. Donald Soper, Baron Soper) (1903-   )

"There is nothing wrong with God; the trouble is with his family."
Calling for Action, page 167

"The fact is that the Bible is an incomparable servant of the truth but an intolerable master."

Calling for Action, page 135

Norman Tebbit, Baron Tebbit of Chingford (1931-   )

"Far better to keep your mouth shut and let everyone think you're stupid than to open it and leave no doubt."

Today, 5 September 1989

George Thomas, 1st Viscount Tonypandy (1909-   )

"I can only say now what I thought as I left Speaker's House for the last time and looked at the portraits of my predecessors: 'I hope I didn't let you down'."

Mr Speaker Thomas, page 230

Horace Walpole, 4th Earl of Orford (1717-1797)

"This world is a comedy to those that think, a tragedy to those that feel."

Bernard Weatherill, Baron Weatherill (1921-   )

"A good speech may not always be remembered but a bad speech is never forgotten — or forgiven."

Independent, 2 May 1992

Duke of Wellington (Arthur Wellesley, 1st Duke of Wellington) (1769-1852)

"I must say that up to the present, the Government have been very successful. There is in fact but little Opposition to it. This state of things cannot last I know."
Elizabeth Longford, *Wellington: Pillar of State,* page 397

John Wheatley (1869-1930)

"If there is no profit in a thing, then the State may have it."
29 November 1922

Lord Whitelaw (William Whitelaw, 1st Viscount) (1918-   )

"The Labour Party is going about the country stirring up apathy."

Shirley Williams (1930-   )

"The saddest illusion of revolutionary socialists is that revolution itself will transform the nature of human beings."

Harold Wilson, Baron Wilson of Rievaulx (1916-   )

"I'm an optimist, but I'm an optimist who takes his raincoat."
1976

"The Monarchy is a labour-intensive industry."
Observer, 13 February 1977

"A week is a long time in politics."
The Labour Government, 1964-70

CHAPTER FIVE

The Way I See It

Many of the comments in the last chapter became part of the common currency of the language only because time has proved their accuracy. Given that political forecasting is the fiefdom of fools, other sayings which have proved false are to be found in the following pages. "I wish I *hadn't* said that" may be the reaction of some quoted here, though few today would boast so blithely of their ignorance as Lord Birkenhead, or be so pessimistic about their influence as Harold Watkinson.

I have allowed myself some partisanship. Some may feel that Attlee on planning deserves a place in "Wit and Wisdom"; but here he is presenting his own view of affairs. So is Baldwin on Europe, or Clarendon on taxes, trade and peace, though I wholeheartedly agree with both. Only time will tell who is right. That Nye Bevan was wrong about Tories doesn't reduce the vigour of his language. Churchill clearly thought books of quotations to be part of a man's education — to learn, perhaps from the wise. There's a gold-mine here as well, waiting to be borrowed, adapted, coloured to your own purpose.

May all your speeches be quotable, and the applause ever music to your ears. No politician could ever ask for more.

Field-Marshal Earl Alexander of Tunis (1891-1969)

Field-Marshal Alexander was notorious for his genuine modesty, even after his great achievements. Visiting old haunts with some friends he went into Maidenhead Boat Club, remarking as he went in, "They may remember me here. I used to be a member once."

Julian Amery, Baron Amery of Lustleigh (1918-   )

"Human nature being what it is, prisons are one of the most fundamental institutions on which society depends."
9 February 1984

Herbert Henry Asquith, 1st Earl of Oxford and Asquith (1852-1928)

"Of all human troubles the most hateful is to feel that you have the capacity of power and yet you have no field to exercise it."
Ross, *Asquith*, page 32

"The army will hear nothing of politics from me and in return I expect to hear nothing of politics from the army."
Speech at Ladybank, 4 April 1914

Asquith had been Home Secretary in Gladstone's last government. During a long and bitter coal strike there had been rioting and troops had fired upon a crowd at Featherstone, killing two miners. Nearly thirty years later he was the candidate for Paisley and was asked "Why did you murder the miners at Featherstone in 1892?" Asquith replied "It was not in 1892, it was in 1893."

Lord Halifax, *The Fulness of Days*, page 247

Nancy, Lady Astor (1879-1964)

"One reason I don't drink is that I want to know when I'm having a good time."

Clement Attlee, 1st Earl Attlee (1883-1967)

"We have shown that orderly planning and freedom are not incompatible."

17 February 1950

Attlee once said that the dilemma facing humanity was because "Man's material discoveries have outpaced his moral progress".

9 November 1945

"If the money wasted on arms could be used to help the less developed nations, that would probably be a greater blow against the Communist danger than anything else."

Kenneth Harris, *Attlee*, page 550

"If you begin to consider yourself solely responsible to a political party, you're half-way to a dictatorship."
Trevor Burridge, *Attlee*, page 191

He also gave a salutary warning to future Chancellors: "It is dangerous to play politics with the Budget."
29 October 1945

Francis Bacon, Viscount St Alban (1561-1626)

"There is little friendship in the world, and least of all between equals."
Essays, 'Of Followers and Friends'

"It is scarcely possible for authors to be admired and at the same time to excel."
Advancement of Learning

"Do not wonder if the common people speak more truly than those of higher rank, for they speak with more safety."
Laus Existimatio

"If only men would be mad in the same fashion and conformably, they might manage to agree fairly well together."
Verba Legis

Stanley Baldwin, 1st Earl Baldwin of Bewdley (1867-1947)

He was in many ways ahead of his time, on one occasion telling a sceptical audience that "Whether we like it or not, we are considerably bound to Europe."

Baldwin described what it was like to be Prime Minister: "It's the loneliest job in the world. A Prime Minister cannot share his ultimate responsibilities."

A.J. Balfour, 1st Earl of Balfour (1848-1930)

"There are plenty of cases of war being begun before it is declared."
12 December 1905

"No country can allow its safety to be wholly dependent on faithful observance by other states of rules to which they are pledged."
25 February 1927

Tony Banks (1940-   )

"The only thing you can be certain about in politics is that you can't be certain about anything."
BBC TV, 10 April 1992

Anthony Wedgwood Benn (1925-)

"I don't want to commit myself in advocating a definite republican constitution which will get bogged down with the question of who would elect the President and when."
Diary, 20 May 1963

"I do not share the general view that market forces are the basis of personal liberty."
22 November 1990

Keith Best (1949-)

"Teaching is a good preparation for politics because you have to reply to questions when you don't know the answer."
Daily Telegraph, 28 December 1991

Aneurin Bevan (1897-1960)

"We should not be pushing out figures when the facts are in the opposite direction."

"What should be the glory of the profession is that a doctor should be able to meet his patients with no financial anxiety."
Hansard, 9 February 1947

"Whenever you scratch a Tory you find a Fascist."

"That is my truth; now you tell me yours." (Favourite saying.)

"'How can wealth persuade poverty to use its political freedom to keep wealth in power?' Here lies the whole art of Conservative politics in the twentieth century."
In Place of Fear, 1952

"The purpose of getting power is to be able to give it away."
Michael Foot, *Aneurin Bevan*, Volume I, Chapter 1

"A Society in which the people's wants do not exceed their possessions is not a Socialist Society."
Michael Foot, *Aneurin Bevan*, Volume I, Chapter 2

"Politics is a blood sport."
Jenny Lee, *My Life With Nye*

Ernest Bevin (1881-1951)

"There has been great excitement at the prospect that this atomic bomb or atomic energy is likely to produce great industrial energy very quickly. I do not believe it at all."
7 November 1945

During a lengthy argument concerning foreign policy and all its intricacies, Bevin became irritated and bellowed out, "My foreign policy is to be able to take a ticket at Victoria Station and go anywhere I damn well please."
Spectator, 20 April 1951

"There has never been a war yet which if the facts had been put calmly before the ordinary folk could not have been prevented. The common man is the greatest protection against war."
1945

Sir William Beveridge, 1st Baron Beveridge (1879-1963)

"I have spent most of my life most happily making plans for others to carry out."
1953

Lord Boothby (Robert, Baron Boothby) (1900-1986)

"No one who had any sense ever liked school."
1983

"I was very precocious. I was pleased with myself. I thought I was very good-looking and I thought I was very clever, and I was."
Daily Express, 6 February 1968

Sir Bernard Braine, Baron Braine of Wheatley (1914-   )

"This House is the grand council of the nation."
22 November 1990

Fenner Brockway, Baron Brockway (1888-1988)

"One cannot even be a good politician if one is less than a complete human being."
Towards Tomorrow, page 262

"I had an unexpected honour at the end of the war. Among Hitler's undestroyed papers was his list of those to be executed when his forces won. It included my name."
Towards Tomorrow, page 144

Edmund Burke (1729-1797)

"Custom reconciles us to everything."
On the Sublime and Beautiful, Part IV

"Bad laws are the worst sort of tyranny."
Speech at Bristol, 1780

"Superstition is the religion of feeble minds."
Reflections on the Revolution in France

"To innovate is not to reform."
A Letter to a Noble Lord

"I do not know the method of drawing up an indictment against a whole people."
House of Commons, 22 March 1775

"You can never plan the future by the past."
Letter to a Member of the National Assembly

"A state without some means of change is without the means of its conservation."
Reflections on the Revolution in France

"To tax and to please, no more than to love and to be wise, is not given to men."
Speech on American Taxation

"Magnanimity in politics is not seldom the truest wisdom; and a great empire and little minds go ill together."
House of Commons, 22 March 1775

"Politics and the pulpit are terms that have little agreement. No sound ought to be heard in the church but the healing voice of Christian charity."
Reflections on the Revolution in France

"The greater the power, the more dangerous the abuse."
House of Commons, 7 February 1771

"Nobody ever made a greater mistake than he who did nothing because he could only do a little."

R.A. Butler, Baron Butler of Saffron Walden (1902-1982)

"I never really got the hang of boiling a kettle." (Apologetic remark to a reporter, explaining why his wife had told him not to make tea in her absence.)
Anthony Howard, *Butler*, page 369

James Callaghan, Baron Callaghan of Cardiff, (1912-   )

"'Your administration will always be noted for the humanity it brought to government'. If that were to be the final epitaph, I should not be unhappy."
Time and Chance, page 398

"Provided we harness progress to morality, there will be room for reasoned optimism for the future."
Time and Chance, page 569

"Heaven on Earth is not tomorrow."
1979

"Memory is a capricious companion."
Time and Chance, Introduction

"When I am shaving in the morning I say to myself that if I were a young man I would emigrate. By the time I am sitting down to breakfast I ask myself 'Where would I go?'"
Barbara Castle, *The Castle Diaries*, Volume I, 1974-76

"What one gets is friendliness but not friendship." (Of his audiences with the Queen.)

Sir Henry Campbell-Bannerman (1836-1908)

"Good government could never be a substitute for Government by the people themselves."
Speech in Stirling, 23 November 1905

"Our view of the public interest leads us to be opposed to this project of a [Channel] tunnel. Even supposing the military dangers involved were to be amply guarded against there would exist, throughout the country, a feeling of insecurity which might lead to a constant demand for increased expenditure, naval and military, and a continual risk of unrest and possibly alarm, which, however unfounded, would be most injurious in its effect, whether political or commercial."
27 November 1887

Edward Cardwell, 1st Viscount Cardwell (1813-1886)

"Let it be known that war with a colony is war with England."

Lucius Carey, 2nd Viscount Falkland (1610-1643)

"When it is not necessary to change, it is necessary not to change."
22 November 1641

J.R. Cartland (1907-1941)

"I have always believed that fear has very little effect upon the conscience of our nation."
22 February 1938

Barbara Castle, Baroness Castle of Blackburn (1911-   )

Mrs Castle was most adept at leaving her readers to decide for themselves: "The Labour Government never abandoned their prices and incomes policy. What they did was to say that the value of a statutory prices and incomes policy had come to an end."
24 March 1971

"I have a haunting feeling there is a silent majority sitting behind its lace curtains, waiting to come out and vote Tory." (The Labour Government lost the next [1970] Election)
The Castle Diaries, Volume II, 1964-70, page 805

Neville Chamberlain (1869-1940)

"In war there are no winners."
24 March 1938

Lord Chesterfield (Philip Stanhope, 4th Earl of Chesterfield) (1694-1773)

"I am sure that since I have had the full use of my reason, nobody has ever heard me laugh."
Letter to his son, 9 March 1748

"Be wiser than other people if you can but do not tell them so."
Letter to his son, 19 November 1745

"Idleness is only the refuge of weak minds."
Letter to his son, 20 July 1749

Lord Randolph Churchill (1849-1895)

"I never could make out what those damned dots meant." (Of decimal points.)

Sir Winston Churchill (1874-1965)

"If we open a quarrel between the past and the present, we shall find that we have lost the future."

"I do not resent criticism, even when for the sake of emphasis it parts for the time with reality."
23 January 1944

"I have democratised cigars."

"It is a good thing for an uneducated man to read books of quotations."
My Early Life, Chapter 9

"The soul of man, frozen in a long night, can be awakened by a spark coming from God knows where and in a moment the whole structure of lies and oppression is on trial for its life. Peoples in bondage need never despair." (Prophesying the end of Communism.)

Martin Gilbert, *Churchill.* BBC TV, 5 Feb 1992

Complaining in 1960, he said: "My life is over, but not yet ended."

Martin Gilbert, *Never Despair*, page 1317

Earl of Clarendon (George William Frederick Villiers, 4th Earl of Clarendon) (1800-1870)

"Foreign policy, Bible societies, corn laws, slave trade and education are matters only of occasional and secondary interest to John Bull, and taxes, trade and peace are what he really cares about."

To Lord Brougham, 13 November 1846

Lord Citrine (Sir Walter Citrine, 1st Baron) (1887-1983)

"The Russians have a habit of making a mystery out of a commonplace."

Two Careers, Volume II, page 309

"'Early to bed and not too early to rise' is my motto."

Sir Edward Coke (1552-1634)

"Magna Carta is such a fellow that he will have no sovereign."
17 March 1628

"How long soever it hath continued if it be against reason, it is of no force in law."

Sir Stafford Cripps (1889-1952)

"We must not allow ourselves to be blinded to long-term developments by the intensity of the short-term difficulties."
7 August 1947

"One should not threaten resignation openly in the Cabinet."

Anthony Crosland (1918-1977)

"Of course, Communists and Trots want Labour to fail."
Susan Crosland, *Tony Crosland*, page 295

Lord Curzon (George Nathaniel Curzon, 1st Marquess Curzon of Kedleston) (1859-1925)

"Personally I do not believe in the likelihood of Persian oil deposits being worked at profit."
Kenneth Rose, *Curzon*, page 234

On seeing some soldiers bathing, Curzon expressed astonishment: "I did not know the lower orders had such white skins."
A.J.P. Taylor, *English History, 1914-45*

"The journalist, whose main duty is speed, is likely sometimes to get advantage over the diplomatist whose main object is accuracy."
Kenneth Rose, *Curzon*, page 316

"The best work in the world was always done by members of the aristocracy."
John Grigg, *Lloyd George: The People's Champion*

Hugh Dalton, Baron Dalton (1887-1962)

"Are not the worst examples of architecture to be found in private enterprise in cheap jerry-built homes?"
28 July 1938

"Some people say 'What would happen if we had a Communist Chancellor of the Exchequer?' I would ask in reply, 'What would happen if we had a lot of Fascist or Mosleyite bank chairmen?' In that event it might be thought disadvantageous to have publicity."
11 December 1945

"One of the most important of all the causes of great inequality of income is the inheritance of a great fortune by a small minority."
Ben Pimlott, *Hugh Dalton*, page 415

"I myself share with the Conservative Party a profound dislike for such fandangles as proportional representation."
29 October 1945

"Unilateralism is not internationalism. It is nationalist egoism gone mad."
Ben Pimlott, *Hugh Dalton*, page 676

Lord Denning (Alfred, Baron Denning) (1899-   )

"This supposed division between the law on one hand and morals on the other has been a great mistake." (On the Profumo scandal.)
Family Star, page 182

"Is it right that we as a society should do a thing — hang a man — which none of us individually would be prepared to do or even witness?"
Family Star, page 165

Lord Derby (Edward Stanley, 14th Earl of Derby) (1799-1869)

On ambition: "Men who make their positions will say and do things which are not necessary to be said or done by those for whom positions are provided."
Richard Muller and James Munson, *Victoria*, page 61

"It bores me to give up translating Homer to talk politics."
Clive Bigham, *The Prime Ministers of Britain*, page 287

Sir Anthony Eden, 1st Earl of Avon (1897-1977)

"All prejudices are equally fatal to good government."

"I dislike our extreme right more than somewhat and I seem for ever to be seeing the other feller's point of view."

"We have many times led Europe in the fight for freedom. It would be an ignoble end to our long history if we tamely accepted to perish by degrees."

"We must not perpetuate an injustice in order to get a little present ease."

"A ready smile concealed a firm mind." (Of Edward Heath).
Full Circle, page 549

Marcia Falkender, Baroness Falkender, (1932-   )

"Personally I agree with Douglas Hurd that champagne, in the evening at least, is better for you, and less expensive than the more commonly consumed hard liquor."
Downing Street in Perspective

Michael Foot (1913-   )

"All is fair in love, war and Parliamentary procedure."

"You can have a wages policy imposed by mass unemployment."

Hugh Gaitskell (1906-1963)

"I can assure you that there is no question of us throwing away the tradition of the Grammar School."
1958

"In the last few years we have learned to distinguish the means of Socialism from the ends."
1950

"We could not have Parliamentary Sovereignty with a European Parliament."
1962

"There are some of us who will fight, fight, and fight again, to save the Party we love." (At the Labour Party Conference in 1960, which voted to support unilateral disarmament.)

"You still hear some people speaking as though we could decide whether the Common Market existed or not."
8 May 1962

Edward Gibbon (1737-1794)

"Fame is the motive, it is the reward for our labours."
Vindication

"Corruption is the most infallible symptom of constitutional liberty."

Sir Ian Gilmour (1926-   )

"The best way of safeguarding the future is by not trying to return to the past."
Inside Right, Part III, Chapter 2

W.E. Gladstone (1809-1898)

"If it shall appear that there is still to be fought a final conflict in Ireland between law on the one side and sheer lawlessness upon the other .... then I say, gentlemen, without hesitation, the resources of civilisation against its enemies are not yet exhausted."
Speech at Leeds, 7 October 1881

"The errors of former times are recorded for our instruction in order that we may avoid their repetition."
Midlothian speech, November 1879

"National injustice is the surest road to national downfall."

"The negation of God erected into a system of government."
(In 1851, of the Government of the King of Naples.)

"Here is my first principle in foreign policy; good government at home." (One of his sayings.)

Lord Goddard (Rayner, Baron Goddard) (1877-1971)

"No one has yet been able to find a method of depriving a British jury of its privilege of returning a perverse verdict."
Observer, 1955

"When a man deliberately murders another he is committing the supreme crime and should pay the supreme penalty."
Fenton Bresler, *Lord Goddard*, page 272

Sir Edward Grey, 1st Viscount Grey of Fallodon (1862-1933)

"Nations are always making mistakes because they do not understand each other's psychology."
Twenty-Five Years, Volume III, page 258

"Indifference is the only state that is incompatible with hope."
Twenty-Five Years, Volume III, page 275

"There is no security for any power unless it be a security in which its neighbours have an equal share."
Twenty-Five Years, Volume III, page 270

"The internal peace of every country depends upon the knowledge that force is available to uphold law."
Twenty-Five Years, Volume III, page 274

Lord Hailsham (Quintin Hogg, Baron Hailsham of St Marylebone) (1907-   )

"Law is, of course, in a sense, no more than a gigantic confidence trick. If enough people did not obey the law it would be totally unenforceable."
The Door Wherein I Went, page 99

"I do not believe that law can exist without sanctions."
The Door Wherein I Went, page 99

"My highest ambition was to become a judge."
The Door Wherein I Went, page 225

"The badge of freedom is variety."
The Door Wherein I Went, page 179

"You cannot practise at the Common Law Bar for more than forty years and be easily shocked."
The Door Wherein I Went, page 197

"It is not always an advantage for a young man to be the son of a prominent person. The forces of inverted snobbery are extremely powerful."

"A politician who enters public life may as well face the fact that the best way of not being found out is not to do anything which, if found out, will cause his ruin."

"I have seen too much of the office of Prime Minister at close quarters to have any illusions that it brings happiness to the recipient."

"The moment politics becomes dull, democracy is in danger."

"The Labour Party of the present is one of the most doctrinaire and bigoted organisations in the world."

Marquess of Halifax (George Savile, 1st Marquess of Halifax) (1633-1695)

"Nothing has an uglier look to us than Reason when it is not on our side."

"A man that should call everything by its right name would hardly pass the streets without being knocked down as a common enemy."

"Men are not hanged for stealing horses but that horses may not be stolen."

"Popularity is a crime from the moment it is sought, it is only a virtue when men have it whether they will or no."

"He who thinks his place below him, will certainly be below his place."

"The memory and conscience never did, nor ever will agree about forgiving injuries."

Sir William Harcourt (1827-1904)

"The Minister exists to tell the Civil Servant what the Public will not stand."
Ian Gilmour, *The Body Politic*, Part II, Chapter 1

Roy Hattersley (1932-   )

"One of the problems of our society is that we spend too much time thinking about punishment and not enough about prevention."
17 December 1990

Denis Healey, Baron Healey (1917-   )

"I have always wanted to do something rather than to be something."
The Time of My Life, page 586

Sir Edward Heath (1916-   )

"Leadership is all about right and wrong."

A.P. Herbert (Sir Alan Herbert) (1890-1971)

"Surely, sir, I can move a dilatory motion." (On being told he had already spoken and exhausted his right to speak.)

Lord Home (Sir Alec Douglas-Home, Baron Home of the Hirsel) (1903-   )

"There are two problems in my life. The political ones are insoluble and the economic ones are incomprehensible."
January 1964

In Cairo, after Nasser's funeral, Lord Home was asked, in view of the great heat, what drink he would like with his ice. He asked what the time was in London, and was told it was 4 o'clock there. "Very well," he said, "I'll have a cup of tea."
Observer, 3 October 1971

Lord Horder (Thomas Horder, 1st Baron) (1871-1955)

"Politicians come and go, but medicine goes on for ever."

Neil Kinnock (1942-   )

"I am the first male member of my family for about three generations who can have reasonable confidence in expecting that I will leave this earth with more or less the same number of fingers, hands, legs, toes and eyes as I had when I was born."
1973
Robert Harris, *The Making of Neil Kinnock*, page 23

"We are at the dawn of the age when the power of democracy is moving out of its single base of the ballot box periodically onto the shop floor."
Robert Harris, *The Making of Neil Kinnock*, page 110

"We have in Britain four raw materials: oil, coal, gas and children."
Robert Harris, *The Making of Neil Kinnock*, page 128

"Unity is the price of victory."
Robert Harris, *The Making of Neil Kinnock*, page 239

"We are the first generation in history to have to deal with the existence of weapons of obliteration .... I would die for my country. But I could never allow my country to die for me." (Explaining his support for the Campaign for Nuclear Disarmament.)

"Long and beautiful." (On being asked what his future would be after Labour's General Election defeat in 1992.)

Henry Labouchère (1831-1912)

"Long Parliaments are as fatal to sound business as long credits are to sound trade." (On the desirability of triennial parliaments.)

Ivan Lawrence (1936-   )

After sitting for hours through a Burton Rugby Club Dinner, during which speech after speech was made to the increasingly alcoholic audience, he was at long last invited by the Chairman to provide a short address. "Grove Farm, Drakelow, Burton-on-Trent," he replied, and left.
Burton Mail

Nigel Lawson, Baron Lawson of Blaby (1932-   )

"There has always been, and there always will be, an economic cycle."
31 October 1989

Sir George Lewis (1806-1863)

"The indiscretion of biographers adds a new terror to death."
Cecil Woodham-Smith, *Florence Nightingale*, page 388

George Lindgren (Baron Lindgren of Welwyn Garden City) (1900-1971)

"Private enterprise is never as safe as State enterprise."
12 November 1947

Ken Livingstone (1945-   )

"I tend to look at modern politics through the perspective of animal behaviour and anthropology which, I should imagine, accounts for why I approach some things differently from other politicians."
Citizen Ken, page 185

Selwyn Lloyd (John Selwyn Brooke Lloyd, Baron Selwyn Lloyd) (1904-1978)

"Politics is the best game in town."
D.K. Thorpe, *Selwyn Lloyd*, page 363

"I am so happy I no longer have to read *The Economist*." (On being dismissed as Chancellor in 1962.)

David Lloyd George, 1st Earl Lloyd George of Dwyfor (1863-1945)

"When one set of people say you are paying too little and another set of people say you are paying too much it rather means you are somewhere about right."
John Grigg, *Lloyd George: The People's Champion*, page 334

Lord Macaulay (Thomas Babington Macaulay, 1st Baron) (1800-1859)

"In every age, the vilest specimens of human nature are to be found among demagogues."

"The object of oratory alone is not truth but persuasion."
Essay, 'On Athenian Orators'

James Ramsay MacDonald (1866-1937)

"The newest block of flats in Park Lane ought to be blown up. But what are we to do? Men of wealth have no idea of how to spend it except for their own vulgar decoration, and Parties that pretend to guard our finer traditions are busy selling them in the market-place."

"We hear war called murder; it is not; it is suicide."
1930

Harold Macmillan, 1st Earl of Stockton (1894-1986)

"Quiet calm deliberation disentangles every knot." (Reportedly, he would mutter this to himself in a crisis.)

"We believe that unless we give opportunity to the strong and able, we shall never have the means to provide real protection for the weak and old."

"I have learned that in all negotiations nothing matters except the will to reach agreement."

John Major (1943-   )

"Nothing makes me more determined to do something than someone telling me I can't."
Nesta Wyn Ellis, *John Major*

"There's a life after politics."
Nesta Wyn Ellis, *John Major*

"I did have some friends at school but I don't know where they are now."
Nesta Wyn Ellis, *John Major*

Lord Mancroft (Stormont Mancroft, 2nd Baron) (1914-1987)

During a conference the subject turned to equality, and to the belief that all men are born equal. Lord Mancroft looked rather dour as he repeated the words "All men are born equal", but his face brightened up as he added, "But quite a few eventually get over it."
Observer, 1967

Christopher Mayhew, Baron Mayhew (1915-   )

"The Labour Moderates go through the motions of revolt and then stay on, giving an air of democratic respectability to political elements which they deeply and rightly distrust."
Time to Explain, page 208

Lord Melbourne (William Lamb, 2nd Viscount Melbourne) (1779-1848)

"It doesn't matter what we all say, so long as we all say the same thing."

"Things have come to a pretty pass when religion is allowed to invade the sphere of private life."

"Damn it all, another Bishop dead — I verily believe they die to vex me."

"Flies are caught with honey, not with vinegar."
Giles St Aubyn, *Queen Victoria*, page 117

John Stuart Mill (1806-1873)

"The perpetual obstacle to human advancement is custom."

Field-Marshal Viscount Montgomery of Alamein (1887-1976)

Just after the Second World War Montgomery did a lecture tour visiting various schools. At the end of one of his lectures, he asked the boys whether they had any questions. A rather timid boy put up his hand and asked Montgomery whom he considered to be the three greatest generals of all time. He replied: "The other two were Alexander the Great and Napoleon."

Lord Moran (Charles Wilson, 1st Baron Moran) (1882-1977)

"A man is as old as his arteries."
Struggle for Survival, page 826

Herbert Morrison, Baron Morrison of Lambeth (1888-1965)

"I should like to be thirty-five and live for ever."
Daily Herald, 3 January 1947

"We want to be friends with all the peoples of the world."
22 February 1938

"He was one of the best Mayors Stepney ever had." (Of Attlee.)
An Autobiography

Sir Gerald Nabarro (1913-1973)

"Educational advance should depend at all levels on qualitative selection."
Nab: Portrait of a Politician, page 323

Tony Newton (1937-   )

"When I am asked by *Who's Who* what my interests are I put DIY and gardening. Then I hope my wife won't read it."
Independent, 3 May 1992

Lord Normanby (Constantine Henry Phipps, 1st Marquess of Normanby) (1797-1863)

"Property has its duties as well as its rights."

Lord Northcliffe (Alfred Harmsworth, 1st Viscount Northcliffe) (1865-1922)

While he was staying at his Broadstairs residence during the Great War, the Germans started shelling the house. A terrified member of his staff came in, shrieking "We will die in our beds". Northcliffe coolly replied "You go and die in yours," and went back to sleep.
Hannan Swaffer, *World Press*, 25 June 1931

Sir Laurence Olivier, Baron Olivier (1907-1989)

"It is just as cold in Westminster Abbey as it is in the village churchyard." (On being asked whether he wanted to be buried in Poets' Corner in Westminster Abbey.)
Anthony Holden, *Olivier*, page 445

Sir Cyril Osborne (1898-1969)

"Peace can come only through strength. It cannot come through pious aspirations or noble speeches."

Dr David Owen, Baron Owen (1938-   )

"I never joined a political party at Cambridge. The nearest I came to doing so was in order to go to a dance. The Liberals were giving it, and if you wanted to go, you had to join their party which you could do at the door. A few of us decided to take a chance and turn up at the door; and while several people were paying their money to join the Liberal Party, we slipped behind their backs and walked into the dance. Had there been more people at the door to take the money, I might have become a Liberal."
Personally Speaking, page 14

Lord Palmerston (Henry Temple, 3rd Viscount Palmerston) (1784-1865)

"We have no eternal allies and we have no perpetual enemies. Our interests are eternal and perpetual and these interests it is our duty to follow."
5 March 1857

"The policy and practice of the Russian Government has always been to push forward its encroachments as fast and as far as the apathy or want of firmness of other Governments would allow it to go, but always to stop and retire when it was met with decided resistance, and then to wait for the next favourable opportunity to make another spring on its intended victim."
1853

"Tenants' right are landlords' wrongs." (One of his sayings.)

The Rev. Ian Paisley (1926-   )

Calling for the return of hanging: "Is it not a fact that the weapon in the armoury of the IRA is capital punishment?"
17 December 1990

Sir Robert Peel (1788-1850)

"However much I have been blamed for not showing more deferences to a great Party, and for not acting more steadily on Party Principles, all I have to regret is that I showed so much."
Norman Gash, *Sir Robert Peel*, page 298

"Considering the sanguinary nature of great battles and that (however just the cause) many thousands forfeit their lives through no fault of their own, to direct a reference to the special intervention of Almighty God is not very seemly."
Norman Gash, *Sir Robert Peel*, page 68

"Much is said about English severity, but not a word about Irish provocation."
From a speech in 1833

"The distinction of being without an honour is becoming a rare and valuable one and should not become extinct."
From a letter to Sir James Graham written in 1841

William Pitt (the Elder), 1st Earl of Chatham (1708-1778)

"Unlimited power is apt to corrupt the minds of those who possess it."
9 January 1770

"Where laws end, there tyranny begins."

William Pitt (the Younger) (1759-1806)

"Necessity is the plea for every infringement of human freedom. It is the argument of tyrants, it is the creed of slaves."
18 November 1783

"England has saved herself by her exertions, and will, I trust, save Europe by her example."

Enoch Powell (1912-   )

"People are disposed to mistake predicting troubles for causing troubles and even for desiring troubles." (After his "rivers of blood" speech led to accusations of fomenting racism.)
20 April 1968

"The function of statesmanship is to provide against preventable evils."
20 April 1968

Ernest Pretyman (1860-1931)

"Great leaders of the Parties are not elected, they are evolved."
(To the Conservative Parliamentary Party.)
21 March 1921

Francis Pym, Baron Pym (1922-   )

"Maybe we should ask the Falklanders how they feel about a war."
Hugo Young, *One of Us*, page 272

Lord Reith (John Reith, 1st Baron Reith of Stonehaven) (1889-1971)

"I was never a dictator because I could always be sacked." (Of himself at the BBC.)

"I doubt I have ever been young."
Jo Grimond, *Memoirs*, page 289

"Anything over six foot two is an affliction." (Of his height.)
Face to Face, BBC TV, 1960

Nicholas Ridley, Baron Ridley of Liddesdale (1929-   )

Asked in 1991 when he thought the Prime Minister should call an election and "go to the country", he replied, "I go to the country each weekend."

Lord Rosebery (Archibald Primrose, 5th Earl of Rosebery) (1847-1929)

"Long after the words that we utter in the hurry of the moment are buried in oblivion by us they are cherished and brought up against us by the nations they offend."
S.H. Jeyes, *Lord Rosebery*, page 261

"A man will blithely do in politics what he would kick a man downstairs for in ordinary life."
Robert Rhodes James, *Rosebery*, Chapter 12

Bertrand Russell, 3rd Earl Russell (1872-1970)

"It would have been very much better for the world [in 1914] if Britain had remained neutral and the Germans had won a quick victory.   We should have not had either the Nazis or the Communists if that had happened."
Face to Face, BBC TV, 1959

"Fanaticism is the danger of the world and always has been and has done untold harm. I think fanaticism is the greatest danger there is. I might almost say I am fanatically against fanaticism."
Face to Face, BBC TV, 1959

"A school is like the world: only government can prevent brutal violence."
Autobiography, Volume II, page 154

"I was in an aeroplane and I said 'Get me a seat in the smoking part because if I can't smoke I shall die.' And sure enough there was an accident and all the people in the non-smoking part drowned. The people in the smoking part jumped into the Norwegian fjord where we landed and were saved. So I owe my life to smoking."
Face to Face, BBC TV, 1959

"I met T.S. Eliot after the beginning of the First World War in London. I said 'Hello, what are you doing here?' He said 'I have just returned from Berlin.' I said 'What do you think of the war?' He said 'I don't know except that I'm not a pacifist.' I said 'I see. You don't care what people are killed about so long as they are killed.'"
Barry Feinberg and Ronald Kasrils, *Dear Bertrand Russell*, page 186

"It is not error which is a danger to independence of mind. It is unwillingness to question everything."
Barry Feinberg and Ronald Kasrils, *Dear Bertrand Russell*, page 108

"Most parents are of the opinion that there is something shameful about the method by which they have brought their children into the world."
Barry Feinberg and Ronald Kasrils, *Dear Bertrand Russell*, page 149

"Those who in principle oppose birth control are either incapable of arithmetic or else in favour of war, pestilence and famine as permanent features of human life."
Some Prospects Cheerful or Otherwise

When he was imprisoned as a conscientious objector in the First World War, Russell told of an encounter he had with the warder at the gate who had to take his particulars. The warder asked what Russell's religion was, and received the reply, "Agnostic". The perplexed man next asked how to spell it, then remarked with a sigh, "Well, there are many religions but I suppose they all worship the same God."

Lord John Russell (1st Earl Russell) (1792-1878)

"If peace cannot be maintained with honour it is no longer peace."

Lord Salisbury (Robert Cecil, 3rd Marquess of Salisbury) (1830-1903)

"We are part of the Community of Europe and we must do our duty as such." (Speech at Caernarvon, 10 April 1888; quoted by the Queen speaking to the European Parliament, May 1992.)

Lord Salisbury (James Gascoyne-Cecil, 4th Marquess of Salisbury) (1861-1947)

"It is much easier to destroy wealth than to destroy poverty but poverty is the enemy, not wealth."
Post-War Conservative Policy, 1942

Hugh Scanlon, Baron Scanlon (1913-   )

"Liberty is conforming to the majority."
Observer, 1977

Gillian Shephard (1940-   )

"Nobody knows me. Why should they? I just tell people I'm the one that looks like Edwina Currie." (On her appointment as Secretary of State for Employment, 1992.)

Richard Brinsley Sheridan (1751-1816)

"A man may think an untruth as well as speak one."

Emmanuel Shinwell, Baron Shinwell (1884-1986)

"I am not concerned about a little inflation."
Hansard, 24 May 1938

"I certainly did not say I would refuse to employ anybody because he had expressed himself in a hostile manner towards nationalisation. What I said was that I would not appoint somebody to a board if he had expressed himself as being against the provisions of the Bill and had declared that nationalisation was bound to prove a failure."
23 June 1947

Sydney Silverman (1895-1968)

"Parliament cannot be a rubber stamp."
Hughes, *Sydney Silverman,* page 168

Sir John Simon, 1st Viscount Simon (1873-1954)

"As long as I get the revenue I stand neutral." (When he was Chancellor of the Exchequer.)
Hansard, 15 February 1938

F.E. Smith, 1st Earl of Birkenhead (1872-1930)

"I am one of the few who have attempted to take part in the farming debate uncontaminated by any expert knowledge in agriculture."
2nd Earl of Birkenhead, *Lord Birkenhead,* Volume II, page 87

Philip Snowden, 1st Viscount Snowden (1864-1937)

"Bolshevism run mad." (Of the Labour Party in 1931.)

Lord Soper (The Rev. Donald Soper, Baron Soper) (1903-   )

"Quite the most Christian thing that has happened in my lifetime is the Welfare State."
C. Thompson, *Donald Soper,* page 197

"I am a lay Lord." (Lord Soper is the leading Methodist of his time, in a House of Lords which has twenty-six Anglican bishops.)
C. Thompson, *Donald Soper*

Alfred, Lord Tennyson (1809-1892)

"He makes no friend who never made a foe."
The Idylls of the King

Margaret Thatcher, Baroness Thatcher of Kesteven (1925-   )

"It's a funny old world." (On her resignation as Prime Minister.)

"Never forget how workers had to beg for the right to work."
Hugo Young, *One of Us*, page 130

"I make up my mind about people in the first ten seconds and I very rarely change it."
Hugo Young, *One of Us*, page 162

"Oh, those poor shopkeepers." (On first seeing the Toxteth riots in 1981.)
Hugo Young, *One of Us*, page 239

"It is a very small world except for the Pacific, which is rather a big place."
Hugo Young, *One of Us*, page 400

"When you hold back the successful you penalise those who need help."
Penny Junor, *Margaret Thatcher*, page 179

"It must be conviction government. As Prime Minister, I couldn't waste time having any internal arguments."
Penny Junor, *Margaret Thatcher*, page 132

"I don't like it if people say one thing in private and another in public."
Patrick Murray, *Margaret Thatcher*, page 208

"Home is the place you go to when you have nothing better to do."
Interview in the USA, 1991

"Many of our troubles are due to the fact that our people turn to politicians for everything."

"I wouldn't say I am driving. I am helping, helping. I hope most effectively."
During the 1992 election campaign, which was led by her successor.

"I am extraordinarily patient provided I get my way in the end."
Observer, 4 April 1989

"You don't tell deliberate lies but sometimes you have to be evasive."
1976

"When you have spent half your political life dealing with humdrum issues like the environment it's exciting to have a real crisis on your hands." (Of the Falklands War of 1982.)
Hugo Young, *One of Us*

"How could we invest for the future or support the wonderful artists and craftsmen whose work also glorifies God unless we had just worked hard and used our talents to create the necessary wealth?"
Hugo Young, *One of Us*, page 425

William Thorne (1857-1946)

"Why is it that big Income Tax payers can get out of their obligations and little men like myself cannot slip through at all?"

Harold Watkinson, 1st Viscount Watkinson (1910-   )

"Politicians cannot alter trends."
Lord Birkenhead, *Walter Monckton*, page 276

Field-Marshal Earl Wavell of Cyrenaica (1883-1950)

"We have the responsibility without the power." (On the last stages of British rule in India, of which he was the penultimate Viceroy.)
Sarah Bradford, *George VI*, page 526

Duke of Wellington (Arthur Wellesley, 1st Duke of Wellington) (1769-1852)

"One gets bored in boring others."
Elizabeth Longford, *Wellington: Pillar of State*, page 397

"I don't know what effect these men will have on the enemy, but by God, they frighten me." (Of his troops.)

"A great country ought not to make little wars."
Clive Bigham, *The Prime Ministers of Britain*, page 198

"I have no time to do what is not right." (His description of diplomacy.)
Clive Bigham, *The Prime Ministers of Britain*, page 199

"Which way does it go on?" (Of the Insignia of the Order of the Garter.)

Ellen Wilkinson (1891-1947)

"Unemployment is bigger than a political party. It is a national danger and a national scandal."
Betty Vernon, *Ellen Wilkinson*, page 143

"Free milk will be provided in Hoxton and Shoreditch, in Eton and Harrow. What more social equality can you have than that?"
Betty Vernon, *Ellen Wilkinson*, page 2?4

"The higher IQs will become intolerable little wretches if stamped from eleven as being superior."
Betty Vernon, *Ellen Wilkinson*, page 223

Ted Willis, Baron Willis (1918-   )

"I have long held the view that the whole country would benefit from a moratorium on new legislation for at least two years."
Evening All, page 189

Harold Wilson, Baron Wilson of Rievaulx (1916-   )

"If the Tories get in, in five years no one will be able to afford to buy an egg." (Remark after someone threw an egg at him.)

"The only limits of power are the bounds of belief."
Michael Korda, *Power in the Office*

CHAPTER SIX

Painting a Pretty Picture

Politicians who master the rich language of simile and metaphor often produce memorable images. Somehow Sir Geoffrey Howe never again recovered his gravitas after Denis Healey's jibe about dead sheep; Disraeli's description of the Government front bench opposite as 'exhausted volcanoes' destroyed their credibility as it entered history.

The TV programme *Spitting Image* showed how powerful a satirical picture can be. David Steel long held that he was never regarded as equal to Dr David Owen in the 1987 election (in which they jointly led 'The Alliance' to defeat) after his TV puppet repeatedly portrayed him as small and ineffective beside a sardonic and contemptuous Doctor. Margaret Thatcher was always (in later years) shown dressed as a man. Norman Tebbit was shown in a biker's thuggish leather jacket, rather than as the 'semi-housetrained polecat' of Michael Foot's description — perhaps because few of us would recognise such a beast.

All this being so, it is surprising that few of today's politicians use word pictures. Perhaps ignorance of how to go about it, in these days when rhetoric is no longer taught in schools, or hesitation in using vivid language for fear of "going over the top" lies behind the flaccid style of many speeches. Television is also to blame — its use of 15-second sound-bites needing only a punchline eliminates the possibility of a witty image carefully built over several minutes.

Euphemism and its partner, understatement, are however, alive and well and, as Eden's remark about Suez shows, have been for some time. Toning down the colours is a necessary art for all politicians; pretending a disaster didn't happen is just one of the tools of the trade. But oh! for florid hyperbole just occasionally. John Major was surely being a little over-cautious when, asked what he thought of the magnificent Pavarotti concert in Hyde Park in 1991, he answered 'It was very nice'.

Lord Aberdeen (George Gordon, 4th Earl of Aberdeen) (1784-1860)

"It must be owned that a victory is a fine thing, but one should be at a distance to appreciate it."
Sir Arthur Gordon, *Lord Aberdeen*, page 31

Clement Attlee, 1st Earl Attlee (1883-1967)

"I think the British have the distinction above all other nations of being able to put new wine into old bottles without bursting them."
Time, 6 November 1950

Francis Bacon, Viscount St Alban (1561-1626)

"All colours will agree in the dark."
Essays, 'Of Unity in Religion'

"Money is like muck, not good except it be spread."
Essays, 'Of Seditions and Troubles'

Stanley Baldwin, 1st Earl Baldwin of Bewdley (1867-1947)

After he had beaten Lord Curzon for the leadership of the Conservative Party — and thus the Premiership — in 1923, Baldwin recorded "I met Curzon in Downing Street from whom I got the sort of greeting a corpse would give to an undertaker."

"Once I leave I leave. I am not going to speak to the man on the bridge and I am not going to spit on the deck." (On retiring from public office.)

Lord Beaverbrook (William Maxwell Aitken, 1st Baron Beaverbrook) (1879-1964)

"The House of Lords is the British Outer Mongolia for retired politicians."

Anthony Wedgwood Benn (1925-   )

"[The Tories] think that they are witnessing the retirement of a popular headmistress under circumstances that some might regret." (On Mrs Thatcher's resignation.)
22 November 1990

Aneurin Bevan (1897-1960)

"Listening to a speech by Neville Chamberlain is like paying a visit to Woolworths; everything in its place and nothing above sixpence."

"Attlee seemed determined to make a trumpet sound like a tin whistle."

Lord Boothby (Robert, Baron Boothby) (1900-1986)

"The Government before the war, presided over successively by Mr Baldwin and Mr Neville Chamberlain, reduced a great country and a great empire from a position of absolute security and world power to the brink of total destruction within a decade! It took the Roman Empire two hundred years of quite enjoyable decadence to achieve the same result."
The Valiant Years, BBC TV, 1960

Lord Boyd-Orr (John, 1st Baron) (1880-1971)

"If people have to choose between freedom and sandwiches, they will take sandwiches."

John Bright (1811-1889)

"The angel of death has been abroad throughout the land. You may almost hear the beating of his wings."

John Burns (1858-1943)

"Every drop of the Thames is liquid history."

R.A. Butler, Baron Butler of Saffron Walden (1902-1982)

"I think the Prime Minister has to be a butcher and know the joints."
1966

Lord Byron (George Gordon Noel Byron, 6th Baron) (1788-1824)

"Hope to merit Heaven by making earth a Hell."
Childe Harold's Pilgrimage, Canto I, stanza 20

James Callaghan, Baron Callaghan of Cardiff (1912-   )

"A lie can be half way round the world before the truth has got its boots on."
The Times, 1976

"The surtax payers, having been soaked, have found a way of getting out of the rain."
18 July 1947

"My Right Honourable friend is advised that to disregard a 'Keep Left' sign is an offence."
4 November 1947

George Canning (1770-1827)

"Black's not so black nor white so *very* white."
New Morality

Sir Winston Churchill (1874-1965)

"By noon it was clear that the Socialists would have a majority. At luncheon my wife said to me 'It may well be a blessing in disguise'. I replied, 'At the moment it seems quite effectively disguised'." (Of the General Election of 1945, which Labour won.)

The Second World War, Volume VI, 'Triumph and Tragedy'

"A fanatic is one who can't change his mind and won't change the subject."

"We hope to see a Europe where men of every country will think as much of being a European as of belonging to their native land, and that without losing any of their love and loyalty of their birthplace."

Amsterdam, 9 May 1948

Earl of Clarendon (George William Frederick Villiers, 4th Earl of Clarendon) (1800-1870)

"Why are Tories like walnuts? Because they are troublesome to Peel."

13 June 1843

John Clynes (1869-1949)

"A Communist is no more a left-wing member of the Labour Party than an atheist is a left-wing member of the Christian Church."

Sir Stafford Cripps (1889-1952)

"I have never found a valuer yet who cannot force up the value of anything in making a claim."
31 January 1938

Hugh Dalton, Baron Dalton (1887-1962)

"I don't want soiled bedclothes." (On being offered the Foreign Office when Ernest Bevin retired.)
1951

Lord Derby (Edward Stanley, 14th Earl of Derby) (1799-1869)

"I kept the cripples on their legs." (Of Palmerston's Government.)
1859
Clive Bigham, *The Prime Ministers of Britain*, page 280

"A leap in the dark ... shooting Niagara." (Of the 1867 Reform Bill.)

Benjamin Disraeli, Earl of Beaconsfield (1804-1881)

"We cannot eat the fruit while the tree is in blossom."
Alroy, 1833

"As I sat opposite the Treasury bench the Ministers reminded me of one of those marine landscapes not very unusual on the coast of South America. You behold a range of exhausted volcanoes. Not a flame flickers on a single pallid crest. But the

situation is still dangerous. There are occasional earthquakes and ever and anon the dark rumbling of the sea."
Manchester, 3 April 1872

"If a traveller were informed that such a man were leader of the House of Commons, he may well begin to comprehend how the Egyptians worshipped an insect." (Of Lord John Russell.)

Sir Anthony Eden, 1st Earl of Avon (1897-1977)

"We are not at war with Egypt. We are in an armed conflict." (Of the Suez Crisis of 1956.)

"The marked victim of the garrotter is not to be condemned if he strikes out before the noose is round his throat."
Full Circle, page 253

"Drift is the demon of democracy."
Full Circle, page 509

Michael Foot (1913-   )

"I asked the simple question whether it was really Mr Tebbit's desire always to give his imitation of a semi-housetrained polecat. The Animal Welfare Society sent me some complaints, but that's another matter."
Another Heart, page 136

SALLY TOWNSEND

Catherine Gladstone (1813-1900)

When Mr Gladstone was defeated in 1886 a visitor to Mrs Gladstone commiserated, "The elections are beyond man's understanding and the course of events can only be guided by the One above."

"Oh, yes," agreed Mrs Gladstone, "and if you wait he'll be down to tea in five minutes."
Elizabeth Longford, *Victoria, R.I.*, page 492

Joe Gormley, Baron Gormley (1917-   )

"The tragedy of Britain is that we have handled our national inheritance with the careful husbandry of the Prodigal Son and the long-term strategy of the Grand Old Duke of York."
Battered Cherub, page 199

Sir Edward Grey, 1st Viscount Grey of Fallodon (1862-1933)

"The lamps are going out all over Europe; we shall not see them lit again in our lifetime."
August 1914

"The ideal Government minister may well be someone who has no itch to run other people's lives."

Lord Hailsham (Quintin Hogg, Baron Hailsham of St Marylebone) (1907-)

"When one becomes Pope, however fortuitously, one owes one's flock a special duty to avoid unorthodoxy." (On keeping to the party line as a Cabinet Minister.)
The Door Wherein I Went, page 109

Denis Healey, Baron Healey (1917-)

"Being attacked by Geoffrey Howe is like being savaged by a dead sheep."
December 1978

"Karl Marx himself preferred a glass of claret to the mug of tea affected by some of his recent converts."
The Time of my Life, page 584

"Though her vindictiveness towards her enemies was unrelenting, Mrs Thatcher was as capricious as Catherine the Great in picking up and dropping her favourites."
The Time of My Life, page 584

"The great she-elephant — she has an impenetrably thick hide, she is liable to mount charges in all directions and she is always thinking on the trot." (Of Mrs Thatcher.)
Patrick Cosgrave, *Margaret Thatcher*, page 166

Sir Edward Heath (1916-   )

"The unacceptable face of capitalism."* (On Tiny Rowland and Lonrho.)
1973

Sir Geoffrey Howe, Baron Howe of Aberavon (1926-   )

Just before Mrs Thatcher resigned, she referred to herself as the Captain of the Cricket Team. In a devastating speech in November 1990, Sir Geoffrey Howe said: "It is rather like sending your opening batsmen to the crease, only for them to find that their bats have been broken before the game by the team captain." (This speech was said to have taken Lady Howe ten years to write, and her husband ten minutes to deliver.)

Neil Kinnock (1942-   )

On Mrs Thatcher's fall, Neil Kinnock was reported to have said that "When you see the way she was done down, you are bound to think that the people who organised the coup must have had a conscience bypass."
Guardian, 19 August 1991

"If I was in the gutter, which I am not, he'd still be looking up at me from the sewer." (Of Michael Heseltine.)
Robert Harris, *The Making of Neil Kinnock*, page 20

---

*It has been said that this much-used expression was in fact the result of a typing error in the final version of Heath's speech, 'face' being inadvertently substituted for 'facets'.

Kinnock described the Alliance of the Liberal Party with the Social Democrats in 1986 as "Liquid grease that slips and slides to the lowest level of responsibility".

David Lloyd George, 1st Earl Lloyd George of Dwyfor (1863-1945)

"An aristocracy is like cheese; the older it is the higher it becomes."
Speech, December 1910

"You cannot feed the hungry on statistics."

"To anyone with politics in his blood this place is like a pub to a drunkard." (To Robert Boothby, of the House of Commons.)
Lord Boothby, *Boothby: Recollections of a Rebel,* Chapter 2

"Doctrinaires are the vultures of principle. They feed upon principle after it is dead."
Dingle Foot, in the *Guardian,* 17 January 1963

Lord Longford (Francis Pakenham, 7th Earl of Longford) (1905-   )

"A prisoner is not the sort of chap the average man would be keen on taking into his club."

Lord Macaulay (Thomas Babington Macaulay, 1st Baron) (1800-1859)

"Many politicians of our time are in the habit of laying it down as a self-evident proposition that no people ought to be free 'till they are fit to use their freedom. The maxim is worthy of the fool who resolved not to go into the water 'till he had learnt to swim."

James Ramsay MacDonald (1866-1937)

"It is not God but the Devil who is in charge of the international situation and those who are working for God in it are poor servants if all they do is to worship God and neglect their duty to circumvent the Devil."

Sir James Mackintosh (1765-1832)

"The Commons, faithful to their system, remained in a wise and masterly inactivity."
Vindicae Gallicae

Lady Dorothy Macmillan (1900-1966)

Lady Macmillan: "I have been rung up by a young man from the Foreign Office with a short black coat and fancy pants."

Harold Macmillan: "How on earth can you tell what he wore?"

Lady Macmillan: "Oh, he spoke like it."

Alistair Horne, *Macmillan*, Volume II, page 315

Harold Macmillan, 1st Earl of Stockton (1894-1986)

"Political death is always uncomfortable, but in my case it could not have been more untimely."
Memoirs, Volume VI, 'At the End of the Day', page 505

"The missionaries of a party, like those of the church, must be well informed as well as enthusiastic."
Memoirs, Volume III, 'Tides of Fortune', page 299

"Mind your own business, but mind how it affects my business too." (To the South African Parliament.)
3 February 1960.

"'Stop-Go' seemed more sensible than using the brake and accelerator at the same time — a practice that later became fashionable."
Memoirs, Volume IV, 'Riding the Storm 1956-59', page 7

"I felt that one head on a charger was enough. Two was more than England's honour would support." (On Eden's resignation after Suez.)

"It isn't those who are always addressing each other as comrade who necessarily show the most brotherly feelings."
Memoirs, Volume IV, 'Riding the Storm 1956-59', page 202

"I once heard of a young man who sat for his matriculation exam and failed. He sat twenty times and every time he failed. But was he discouraged? Not a bit of it. He set up in business as a crammer and advertised 'Coaching for the Matric — Twenty

Years' Experience'. And I believe he did very well. Afterwards he set up as a Socialist leader."
Memoirs, Volume IV, 'Riding the Storm 1956-59', page 352

"The most striking of all the impressions I have formed ... is of the strength of this African national consciousness ... The wind of change is blowing through this continent." (Speech to the South African Houses of Parliament.)
3 February 1960

John Major (1943-   )

"The people who make quantum leaps only have backwards to go."
Nesta Wyn Ellis, *John Major*, page 81
"If I accurately recall my Shakespeare: 'You draweth out the thread of your verbosity finer than the staple of your argument' — appropriately from *Loves Labour's Lost.*" (To Neil Kinnock.)
13 March 1992

Sir Richard Marsh, Baron Marsh (1928-   )

"There is a popular belief among Prime Ministers that regular bursts of activity make it look as if something positive is happening."

Lord Melbourne (William Lamb, 2nd Viscount Melbourne) (1779-1848)

"While I cannot be regarded as a pillar, I must be regarded as a buttress of the church, because I support it from outside."

Daniel O'Connell (1775-1847)

"Peel's smile, like the silver plate on a coffin."
26 February 1835

Lord Palmerston (Henry Temple, 3rd Viscount Palmerston) (1784-1865)

"You may call it coalition, you may call it the accidental and fortuitous concurrence of atoms."
5 March 1857

Sir Robert Peel (1788-1850)

In 1841, Sir Robert Peel watched scornfully as the Chancellor of the Exchequer introduced his budget, a scene — and perhaps sentiments — felt so often since. "Can there be a more lamentable picture than that of a Chancellor of the Exchequer seated on an empty chest by a pool of bottomless deficiency fishing for a budget?"

Enoch Powell (1912-   )

"Of all political sacred cows, education is the most sacred and the most cow-like."
June 1968

Lord Rosebery (Archibald Primrose, 5th Earl of Rosebery) (1847-1929)

"We regard our parties as interesting groups of gladiators."
S.H. Jeyes, *Lord Rosebery*, page 261

Bertrand Russell, 3rd Earl Russell (1872-1970)

"I cannot claim that my pen has been mightier or even busier than other people's swords."
The Archive of Bertrand Russell, Preface

Lord Salisbury (Robert Cecil, 3rd Marquess of Salisbury) (1830-1903)

"A gram of experience is worth a ton of theory."
Saturday Review, 1859

Lord Shaftesbury (Anthony Ashley Cooper, 7th Earl of Shaftesbury) (1801-1885)

"An iceberg with a slight thaw on the surface." (Of Peel.)
Herbert Van Thal, *The Prime Minister*, page 383

F.E. Smith, 1st Earl of Birkenhead (1872-1930)

"All political parties have skeletons in their cupboard, some with manacles on, some with their hands tied behind their backs."
2nd Earl of Birkenhead, *Lord Birkenhead*, Volume I, page 152

"I appeal to the House to resist the temptation of laying up for themselves treasure in Heaven by the inexpensive method of confiscating other people's treasure on earth."
2nd Earl of Birkenhead, *Lord Birkenhead*, Volume I, page 188

Lord Soper (The Rev. Donald Soper, Baron Soper) (1903-   )

"I as a Methodist must look at the Prayer Book very much as the pious look at the harp; though not much involved with it at the moment they hope to be much more involved with it later on."
C. Thompson, *Donald Soper*, page 199

"What is the difference between putting a baby on the fire and putting the fire on the baby? Surely the answer is the anonymity of 25,000 feet." (Speaking against the Vietnam War.)
C. Thompson, *Donald Soper*, page 202

Margaret Thatcher, Baroness Thatcher of Kesteven (1925-   )

"Standing in the middle of the road is very dangerous, you get knocked down by the traffic from both sides."
Lord Prior, *Balance of Power*

Lord Thurlow (Edward, 1st Baron Thurlow) (1731-1806)

"Corporations have neither bodies to be punished, nor souls to be condemned, they therefore do as they like." (Usually quoted as "Did you ever expect a corporation to have a conscience, when it has no soul to be damned, and no body to be kicked?")

Duke of Wellington (Arthur Wellesley, 1st Duke of Wellington) (1769-1852)

On being asked how to deal with an unruly mob, Wellington's formula was that "Force should be applied in one direction and as many avenues for escape left open as possible."
Neville Thompson, *Wellington after Waterloo*, page 253

Harold Wilson, Baron Wilson of Rievaulx (1916-   )

"You must understand that I am running a Bolshevik Revolution with a Tsarist Shadow Cabinet."   (To Richard Crossman.)
12 March 1963

"The Labour Party is like a stage-coach. If you rattle along at great speed everybody is too exhilarated or too seasick to cause any trouble. But if you stop everybody gets out and argues about where to go next."